Basildon

memories

Basildon

memories

Jim Reeve

TEMPUS

Frontispiece: Aerial photograph of Basildon, 1939.

First published 2006

Tempus Publishing Limited
The Mill, Brimscombe Port,
Stroud, Gloucestershire, GL5 2QG

British Library Cataloguing in Publication Data.
A catalogue record for this book is available from the British Library.

ISBN 0 7524 3819 0

Typesetting and origination by Tempus Publishing Limited
Printed in Great Britain

Contents

Acknowledgements

I would like to thank the many people who have assisted me in compiling this book and have generously given me their time, shared their life experiences and loaned me their precious photographs. I would especially like to mention Denise Rowling of Laindon Library who willingly made her collection of photographs (which she had collected over seven years) available to me, plus the staff at Basildon Library who have been so helpful. Their knowledge of the town has been invaluable; I would also like to thank Basildon District Council, Basildon Development Corporation and the Staff at the Essex Records Office for their help, Fords, Ilfords, Bill Cox of Basildon History website and the following people, without whom this book would not have been possible. Bob and Joy Ayres, Sandra Bonnett, Fred and Thelma Broom, Margaret Browning, Mark Francois MP, Bob and Janet Garrard, Elsie Hill, Roy Ives, Margaret Jackson, Janet Millwood, Betty Morley, David and Gayle Pratt, Albert Lee, Ken and Carol Porter, Rosie Powell of Ilfords, Pat and John Radley, Tony and Maureen Read, Horace and Olive Remmington, John and Ann Rugg, Maud Sargeant, the late Yvonne Smith, John Snoding, Jim and Sadie Turnbull, Vic York, Roy Wallis, life-time friend, Rose Wright and Olive Norfolk for her assistance in research and my editor Cate Ludlow for her great help and assistance. I apologise to the many people of organisations that could have been included in the book but unfortunately I was restricted by space.

I would like to say a special thank you to my son Paul who is a computer wizard and transferred my photographs onto disc, and last but by no means least, Joan, my wife, who came with me on most of the visits and without whose help this project would never have been completed.

Introduction

During the war, when I was a child in Rawreth, I don't recall hearing the name Basildon. It was not until the late fifties, after I had left the police force and had joined Leyton Borough Council as a housing assistant, that I learned of this place in Essex called Basildon where they were going to build one of the new towns. Our housing applicants could apply for a new house in Basildon in two ways. One was to find a job in Basildon and ask their prospective employers to nominate them for housing. The other was to be a key worker for one of the many firms that had transferred to a new site in Basildon. York Borg was an example of this when they brought thirty key workers down from Nottingham, including Mr and Mrs Garrard. I did not know at that time that six years later I would obtain a post in the Housing Department of Basildon Development Corporation, and can remember in 1967 the wonderful feeling of open space and fresh air while walking around the new properties in Vange and the enchantment of the plotlands while collecting rents. I could not help comparing the experience with the rundown housing stock of Bethnal Green where I had worked for six years. The people of the plotlands, I soon realised, were a special breed and in these places, off the beaten tracks, showed an independence which I admired. They made do with what they had, grew their own vegetables and most had no modern facilities. One I shall never forget was ninety-year-old Mr Davidson, who was not one of our tenants but had a zest for life and was full of enthusiasm. We would talk about fishing and life. He often brought fish into my wife's office and opening his brown case would take out the catch from the night before. He would fish in a boat all night off Southend and then come into her office still full of life.

The architecture and design of the development corporation's estates were good and the architects used great imagination, encouraged by generous grants from the Government of the day to experiment with new building methods but no one could have foreseen the vast social changes that have taken place over the last five decades.

In the book I have recalled, as accurately as I can, the memories of some of the original plotlanders, how they lived, went to school and played. I have also tried to record reminiscences of the newcomers as they arrived in the new town from London and all parts of the country.

In the past, Laindon and Pitsea were more dominant than Basildon. The populations of the Basildon areas following the 1801 census were: Laindon 304, Basildon 62 and Pitsea 211. Today's population according to the 2001 census, is in excess of 165,668. This now of course includes Billericay and part of Wickfod. The reason I have excluded Billericay and Wickford from this book is that these have already been covered in *Wickford Memories* by me and *Billericay Voices* by Sylvia Kent, both published by Tempus.

There is evidence of ancient man having lived in Basildon and the surrounding area and proof of this is the stone hammer of Neolithic Man or Bronze Age Man found in Timberlog Lane. There is also proof of Celts, Saxons and Romans living in the area. The very name of Basildon has Saxon origins in Beorhtel Hill with Pitsea meaning 'the island of the Pic' while Vange means Fen District. When Swanmead School was being built sixty bronze pieces were discovered which were thought to have dated back to between 1000 BC and 750 BC. Fragments of Celtic spear heads and sword blades have been found and Roman tiles and bricks were found near Vange Hall. All these things point to the fact that Basildon was inhabited and has a long history.

Modern Basildon had its roots in the decision of The Land Company in 1891 to buy up land from cash-strapped farmers and sell it on in plots. The farmers had more or less lost the fight with the cheaper imported grain from America and Canada. The Land Company's idea coincided with the expansion of the railways and they teamed up together to organise specially priced trips to Laindon, Pitsea and Wickford. Posters went up in London advertising the benefits of living in the country and must have sounded like heaven to many people living in the slums of the East End. The plots were priced for as little as £10. People came down in droves and were met at the stations by horse and carts which took them out to the farms. There, they were entertained in marquees with a meal and drinks which cost 2s 6d. Once the buyers were in the right frame of mind the sale began. The plots near the stations were the first to be sold but those further out proved more difficult.

After the Londoners had made their purchases, they came down at weekends and holidays, living in bell tents, railway carriage coaches and, as Albert Lee relates, a ship's cabin, in fact, anything to give shelter. Some occupiers gradually built shacks, which they slowly converted into bungalows. Some plots, once purchased, were never visited and taken over by other occupiers which gave the Basildon Development Corporation Legal Department a headache trying to establish ownership.

Interviewing the children of some of these original plotlanders, it becomes very apparent that, although many had been poor, there was a good community spirit where they cared for one another. On Friday nights Laindon and Pitsea stations were teeming with people coming down, loaded with building materials and tools for the weekend's work. The residential plotlanders looked after the weekenders' plots while they were away, ensuring that nothing was stolen. The weekenders also ordered materials from Careys in the High Street and Collings one week, to be there ready for them the following week. On Sunday nights the trains were crowded on the way back to London with passengers carrying flowers, tomatoes, cabbages and potatoes grown on their plots.

Many of the residential plotlanders commuted to London each day, walking through the mud in their wellington boots and leaving them at the station until they returned at night. Some cycled down to the stations, leaving their bikes unlocked all day. At the end of the day, the returning workers were guided home by oil lights left on in their neighbours' windows. These were not turned off until the last person had passed.

The plotlanders concreted strips down the muddy paths wide enough for a pram and laid duck-boards, paying for them by collecting money in boxes left on gates, which were never stolen. The areas were well served with shops. During the 1930s there were 120 shops in Laindon and ninety in Pitsea and Vange.

When war was declared in 1939 the weekend plotlanders came down to escape the bombing in London, many of the women staying while their menfolk, if they were not in the Forces, stayed in London during the week, coming down at weekends. Unfortunately some of them did not escape completely as over twenty lives were lost and over 6,000 homes were damaged in Essex, some completely demolished. Twenty-six planes were shot down in the area, unfortunately more Allied than German. The enemy planes were following the twisting river Thames on their return journey and jettisoned their bombs on the Essex countryside before heading out over the North Sea.

This idealistic plotland life was brought to a dramatic end by the 1946 New Towns Act, introduced by the Labour Government of the day setting up seven new towns around London. Billericay's councillors saw the proposal of the new town as a way out of the dilemma of unmade roads, housing shortage, unemployment and also a way of increasing the council's revenue. Many of the electorate strongly contested the proposal, forming groups, but despite the strong opposition the Basildon Development Corporation was established and its first chairman, Sir Lancelot Keay, was appointed. It was not long before Basildon became the dominant partner and took over Billericay Council.

Despite the vast increase in population, housing and industry there are still places that the residents requiring tranquillity can escape to – Langdon Hills, Watt Tyler Park, Gloucester Park and a number of smaller recreation areas within car or walking distance. I am amazed at the amount of entertainment within the area from cinemas to a bowling alley, nightclubs to cricket, football, rugby and tennis clubs. Many I have mentioned but some I have had to miss out due to the limitation of space for which I hope they will forgive me.

one

Early Times

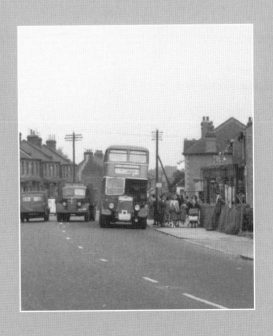

Thomas Helmore

Thomas Helmore was an auctioneer and estate agent who was based at No. 3, Green Street, Upton Park, London and bought up farmland in Laindon, selling it on in plots to Londoners. My father bought a number of plots which covered 365 yards frontage and were situated at the back of where Laindon Centre is now. On the plot, a builder called Patrick, built a wooden four-bedroomed bungalow which we called Dorisdene after my mother Doris.

We drank filtered water which had run off the roof into a well. There were six of us children and mum kept open house. On Saturday evenings during winter we sat round the piano or on the half-sized billiard table and laughed and sung.

Dad helped to feed the whole family on vegetables he grew. He kept ducks, geese, chickens and goats. The goose eggs were delicious and were a meal in themselves.

Roy Ives

Weekends at Laindon

When I was five I will never forget my mother dressing up on a Saturday morning in all her finery, high heels, high hat and two-piece suit in preparation for the journey to the bungalow for the weekend. When we got out at Laindon I can remember the pungent smell of rotting wood and the trek along the two-feet-six-inch concrete pathways on one side of the muddy tracks to our bungalow. The concrete paths had been laid and were maintained by owners of the properties and financed by collections.

Laindon station on Sunday evening was packed with people going back to London but during the summer the trains ran every twenty minutes and were already full by the time they reached us.

Roy Wallis

Basildon Post Office

My relations, Nathan and Rosetta Breadwell, ran Basildon Post Office on the corner of Gardiners Lane and Cranes Farm Road and they resigned in 1895, possibly because the salary was going to be cut. At the time it was five pounds and nine shillings per annum.

Ken Porter

The Golden Dustman of Bethnal Green

My grandfather, Charles Frederic Wallis MM was a dustman on the river Thames. People called him 'the golden dustman' because he had the knack of turning a penny into a pound. By pretending he was a man of means he was elected as a councillor to Hackney Borough Council. He was in the First World War and was

Early poster advertising plots.

Laindon High Road, 1914.

therefore eligible, under the Land Division Act, to apply for a piece of land and was granted a piece in Laindon, where the Gin Factory stands now. The land measured 130yds x 50yds and with the help of his two sons and son-in-law he built a seven-roomed bungalow which they called Lily Villa, after a granddaughter.

In 1927 my grandfather died and my grandmother, aunt and her family moved in, but after a while my grandmother became ill and because of the sanitary arrangements (there was a huge earthenware toilet, which had to be emptied into a deep hole with the rubbish), and my aunt's increasing family, they moved out. Then for a number of years the place lay derelict but when my grandmother died my father opened it up and we used it for weekends and holidays.

Water was collected from the roof and piped into a rough and ready filter made from a compartmentalised set of chambers containing stones, charcoal and gravel. We stored the water in a huge pre-cast concrete bottle set in the ground and it was delicious although at times it had little red water flies swimming around in it.

Roy Wallis

Rubbish Collection

At first our rubbish was bashed, burnt and buried, then in the late forties the council put three big dustbins at South Hill junction which was a disaster. It encouraged rats and flies and so in the seventies, we refused to pay our rates. After time the chairman of the council said he would have the matter investigated and eventually they changed the system.

Elsie Hill (*née* Neville)

Seven Acres of Brambles

We lived in Canning Town where mum gave birth to twins. Unfortunately both died within six weeks. Mum was devastated and would sit in front of the fire staring into the flames. The doctor diagnosed that she was on the verge of a breakdown. Poor dad racked his brains to find a solution to the problem, then one night, he came home full of excitement; an ex-merchant seaman had told him of seven acres of land near his house going for fifty quid. The snag was that it had not been touched for years. One Sunday we went down to have a look at Woodlands in

Dorisdene, Cambridge Road, 1956.

Blind Lane. We ploughed through the mud and blackberry bushes. Mum burst into tears, 'It's seven acres of brambles!'

'That's all right. We'll soon get it sorted' said dad and we spent the next three weekends clearing it and soon we noticed that mum was improving.

Dad had a lot of mates in the Victoria Docks and purchased a stout oak ship's cabin from one of them and brought it back on a lorry he borrowed. At the same time he brought home an old black kitchen range which he rested on four bricks.

Two years later dad started building the bungalow but where to get materials? He came up with the solution when he heard, on the grape vine, that they were pulling down the Old Imperial Music Hall in Old City Road and that all the bricks were stacked in the road. One Saturday morning he pulled up outside the theatre, tipped a policeman to redirect the traffic while he and his mates loaded up the bricks. Dad's firm did not know it but they supplied the timber and slates.

The property still did not have water, electricity, gas, or sewerage but dad soon solved these problems. For water he bought a galvanised tank and filtered the rain water from the roof. For sewerage he purchased an Elsan toilet.

At first we went down at weekends and holidays then our house in Canning Town was bombed and we came down permanently.

Albert Lee

Telephone Exchange

My grandfather, Mr French, lived in property which eventually became the telephone exchange on the corner of Vowler Road. Unfortunately, he and his wife died leaving their three young children to be adopted by an aunt in London.

Ann Rugg (*née* Bullimore)

Elsan Toilet

I loved living on the plotlands. I didn't mind having no electricity or running water but I hated going outside in the dark to the Elsan toilet because it stood by a big plum tree whose leaves and branches cast moving shadows on the walls as you sat there. I could not get out quickly enough. When we had to empty the toilet we moved part of the enormous compost heap and emptied the toilet on it and then covered it.

Maud Sargeant

Collings Shop, Laindon High Road. Note the postmen's uniforms.

They Took the Furniture Van

My grandfather moved down from Plaistow to Rosscombe, a bungalow in Pound Lane. Some time later he invited my parents down and gave them a nearby bungalow as a belated wedding present. The property was built by Stubbs and called Maveri. It had been empty for nearly a year. The weekend war broke out my parents loaded their furniture van and set off from Ilford to their bungalow. When they reached Gallows Corner the army stopped them and commandeered the van piling all the furniture on the roadside and covering it with a tarpaulin. The next day another van was hired to pick up the furniture and complete the journey.

John Rugg

The Long Haul

At weekends and school holidays we came down by train from London. It was exciting as we passed the stations trying to guess which one would win the annual garden competition. On the train there would be lots of weekenders loaded with cases, rexine bags, building materials and short lengths of fishbox wood tied with string. Mum and dad found it a long haul from Laindon Station to our plot at Old Hill Avenue with two small children, a pram, dog, food, tools and building materials. In the end my father thought up the idea of making himself a rope harness which he padded with navy blue serge to protect his neck. Mum would push and he would pull.

Trees arched across the road forming a tunnel while rain-filled ditches ran along- side the road. We used to pass a shop which had a notice saying 'You can telephone from here.' Then we would stop and chat to PC Wells outside the police houses at the bottom of Crown Hill. We would breathe a sigh of relief when we reached Old Hill Avenue and stopped to buy milk straight from the cows at Mr Siburn's farm. During harvest time we often helped him with the harvest. When we reached our plot we hoisted our flag to show we had arrived and then put the kettle on the fire in the bank outside. After we had a meal we would walk to the pond and draw water, which we would boil, cool and then pour into the container.

The return journey on Sunday night was just as exciting, each passenger loaded with flowers and vegetables from their plots.

Elsie Hill (née Neville)

Old Prince of Wales Noak Bridge, possibly 1920.

A Dog Called Rinda

I used to walk for miles with my dog Rinda. On the plotlands we used gas for lighting and cooking but the mantles for the gas lighting were so delicate that if you touched them they fell apart. Our water came straight from the roof into a tank and then through a filter of charcoal, sand and pebbles. Our toilet was an Elsan in the garden.

My dad worked and so we had a man called Mr Brown who came in and cut our grass effort-lessly with a scythe. He would do a couple of sweeps then spit on a sharpening stone and rub it along the long blade. The grass was as neat as it is today with a lawnmower. We had a cow that gave birth to a calf and I remember her crying when they took it away. We also had a chicken called Doodle because it would warn us of approaching doodlebugs by clucking like mad and running for the nearest hedge.

The late Yvonne Smith

Concrete Paths

At first all the roads on the plotlands were mud on which we put duckboards but then the occu-piers decided to do something about it by laying a concrete pathway, wide enough for a pram, all the way down the Cambridge Road.

People kept ducks, chickens, rabbits, geese and bought their animal food from the two corn chandlers, Cramphorns and Simmons.

When we first moved into Wash Road, we had no fences and on our first morning we sat down to breakfast and looked out of our window to see cows staring in.

Roy Ives

Dunton Museum

I was born in Hill Top, Third Avenue, Dunton. My aunt, Mina Mills lived opposite, in the small bungalow which is now the Dunton museum. When we were young we felt safe and would wander for miles.

Maureen Read

Bluebells

As kids we would take our sandwiches and walk through the back lanes to Langdon Hills to pick bluebells. We used to protest if any of the kids

Plotlands bungalow.

pulled the bluebells out by their roots as they would not grow next year.

We played whip and top and hop scotch in the street. While we waited to change buses for Chelmsford Technical School we would go scrumping in a big orchard in Billericay.

Olive Remmington

Unmade Grass Roads

I came down to Laindon when I was about a week old and moved into a bungalow in Cambridge Road. The road was an unmade grass one until my father and a few other residents made a concrete path big enough to wheel a pram down. They were selling plots for £7 and £7 15s. Life was great but everything changed when they started building the new town.

David Pratt

Bucket and Chuck It

My grandparents, Frederick and Beatrice Pitts, with my mother, Hilda and her three sisters moved from Greenwich to Concord in Pound Lane in 1928 and that was where I was born in 1944. The bungalow was built on a small homestead called Salmons Farm. This was one of the homesteads which formed part of Laindon Manor.

Concord had a bucket and chuck it toilet. The bungalow only had cold water and hot water you had to boil up. They moved into the house opposite, called Kia-ora, in 1928. It had a flush toilet even though it was round the back. Dad was one of the few people who had a car and built a garage on the side. He moved into St Nicholas Lane in the 1930s with his parents. My aunt also had a place in Pound Lane called Amelia, which was my grandmother's name.

At the back of Kia-ora were corn fields, where on Guy Fawkes Night, I used to have my bonfire. I would go for miles to collect the wood but our Guy Fawkes nights were spoilt in the 1950s when they built the Pound Lane Estate. As kids, you could wander for miles in safety. All the roads which ran off Pound Lane and St Nicholas Lane were mainly unmade. Basildon Drive and Dickens Drive were plotlands and had unmade roads.

Ken Porter

Howard's Dairy in the 1950s.

Enefer's Cafe

I was born in Scarborough in 1945. When I was eight, we moved to Laindon just as the war ended. Mum, Anne Christensen and dad took over Enefer's cafe at the Fortune of War. We used to have some real characters as customers. After the war, people used to go down to Southend for a day out in their kiss-me-quick hats. The charabancs would call in about 11 a.m. and on the way down, people would grab a cup of tea and a bun. We would stay open until 2 a.m. to catch them coming back. In September, when the Southend lights were on, the coaches would stream in one after another. The passengers poured out and headed straight for the toilets. We had to keep an eye on some of them because they would steal ashtrays, and smash up the toilets. We served them tea and sandwiches and they would queue almost to the door.

I did everything in the cafe, from making 1,000 rolls a day and buckets of ice cream which we made in a factory at the back. We also supplied visiting fun fairs with our ice cream.

The local Laindon people were nice and when I drive through today I see it in my mind's eye as it was, with all the little shops, Hiawatha Corner, the cinema and the War Memorial, which was a drinking fountain. They had good shops and you could buy many things from good clothes and

shoes from Bata and Curtess' shoe shop where Mr Curtess was expert at fitting shoes.

Gayle Pratt

'Knees-up Mother Brown'

When I was ten I became interested in public transport and would go to the Fortune of War to watch the scores of coaches going down to Southend on day trips. My parents forbade me to go across the Arterial Road to the pub because all people went in for was a good time. One day I plucked up the courage and crossed the road and looked through the door. I could not believe it, all these ladies doing a knees-up.

John Rugg

Troubleshooter

There was often trouble at Enefer's cafe especially at two in the morning and I used to sort it out. Although there was a lot of damage we never called the police. I would pick up the broken cups and stop the customers from causing any further damage.

After they had a night in Southend seeing the lights they would want a meal. Tea was two pence halfpenny.

David Pratt

Charabancs at the Fortune of War during the 1950s.

The Fortune of War during the late 1920s.

Gas Lighting

I was born in Ivy Cottage, Worthing Road, Laindon which was opposite the old Manor House. The road was made up and at the bottom were shops and the cinema. There were five of us living in the cottage, mum, dad, my brother, sister and me.

As children, our lives revolved round the Manor Mission who ran various clubs for the youngsters like the Girl Guides, Brownies, Scouts, Christian Endeavour and a games night. They also had a band. The congregation were kind and taught us Christianity.

Basildon Development Corporation loaned the Girl Guides a piece of land at the top of Grove Avenue to use for their activities.

Olive Remmington

The Passing Year

We were very aware of the changing seasons. Winter was the hardest when we worked quickly to get all our tasks finished in daylight hours. We woke early to a very cold house with wonderful patterns on the windows made by Jack Frost. We lit the stoves in the scullery and

Staff at Enefers Cafe, including: Gayle Pratt, Ruth Doc, Mrs Anne Christensen, Mr Christensen, bull dog terrier Peggy, Mrs Lewis, Betty Keeble, Mrs Kendal, Bill Cordey plus dog Bess. Two of the girls were Daggenham pipers.
Mrs Kendal, the lady in the apron on the left, was the one we bought the land off.

Enefers Cafe, Fortune of War, late 1940s.

bedrooms and then put the kettle on which took twenty minutes to boil. We washed in ice cold water or water from the hot-water bottles. We cooked breakfast on an oil stove and then my sister left for the station on her bike, where she would leave it all day at Mr Pepperall's the newsagent for three pence a week. Indoor water containers were filled from the frozen tanks, taps thawed, the toilet emptied and goats milked. At Christmas we gathered holly, ivy and pine cones to paint.

Spring was a time of preparation, planting the crops, looking after the new chicks and goats' kids. We watched in awe and amazement as the plot came to life after the dark days of winter with the dawn chorus and the leaves bursting into life.

Summer was a time of long lazy days admiring our hard work in the garden, relaxing, or taking long walks and seeing visitors.

Autumn was the busiest time, gathering in our crops and preserving fruit. We put all the green tomatoes in shoe boxes between layers of newspapers. We gathered chestnuts and hazelnuts for Christmas. It was a time of produce shows and exchanging ideas.

Elsie Hill (*née* Neville)

Meat on the Book

My father had a butcher's shop in Rectory Road and a lot of people used to have meat on the book, which meant they did not pay for it until they had the money. When the slump came along in 1920 people owed him a lot and he went broke. As a result he joined the Merchant Navy and went to sea. We then moved into Rosemarie Drive for a while and then later to a flat above Norton's furniture shop in Pitsea Road.

Margaret Browning

Shops In Pitsea

The main shopping area was Pitsea Broadway but shops edged most of the High Road starting east of the railway bridge. Once a week at Solly Joels the baker, my sister and I used to wait with a basin in our hand for the arrival of ice cream, collected by van off the London train. George Highwood the butcher was next door to Hickleys garage and further up towards the school was Walter Cook the chandlers where we bought broken biscuits. On the other side of the road was Dearing the shoe mender, Sharps fish shop and Em Johnson the greengrocer. At the eastern end of Pitsea was Cooks the Drapers where we bought our best shoes and clothes.

In Station Lane was Greens the Undertakers. They ran their business from the corner of Hazelmere Drive, now part of the Tesco car park. Whenever, we complained at home of some minor ache or pain the reply would be 'send for Greeny'. Today this expression is still used in our family.

Margaret Jackson

Wickford Market

My dad used to go to Wickford market and buy ducks and chickens. One day he came home with a pig in the back and some ducks and when we got up the next morning all the ducks had flown. He used to keep rabbits and ferrets.

Gayle Pratt

Hiawatha House

My husband Anthony was a doctor from 1963-1998 and at first worked with Dr Long in Hiawatha house. Many of his patients lived on the plotlands and when he visited them he would park his car on the nearest road, put on his wellingtons and walk. The doctors worked a rota for night and weekends and he was frequently called out but in the end they used a deputising service. One day he was called out to the daughter of a family who lived on the plotlands who

Enefer's Cafe, Laindon

⟶ MENU ⟵

BEVERAGES

Tea (per Pot)	3d.
„ China (per Pot) ...	4d.
Coffee (all Milk)	3d.
Horlicks (with Milk) ...	5d.
Cocoa (all Milk)	3d.
Beefex and Biscuit ...	3d.
Soda and Milk	3d.
Glass of Milk	2d.
Minerals ... ... 3d. and 4d.	

BREAD, CAKES, ETC.

Bread & Butter, Brown or White (per portion)	2d.
Roll and Butter	2d.
Scone and Butter ...	2d.
Biscuits (Various) ...	2d.
Toast (per Portion) ...	2d.
Home Made Cake ...	2d.

SWEETS

Fruit Tart (per Portion)	3d.
Cream „ „	2d.
Fruit Salad	5d.
„ „ and Cream	7d.
Peaches Pears Pineapple (per portion)	4d.

SPECIAL

Fish Suppers on Saturdays and Sundays Only.

———

Hot Lunches — Every Day— 12 to 2 p.m. 1/- per head.

SANDWICHES

Cheese	3d.
Ham	4d.
Tongue	6d.
Sardine	4d.

GRILL (10 MINUTES)

Steak and Chips ...	1/3
Chop and Chips ...	11d.
Mixed Grill	1/4
Sausages (Two)	5d.
„ and Chips ...	8d.

SAVOURIES

Steak and Onion Pie and Chips (Home Made)	7d.
Egg and Chips 7d. Two	9d.
Scrambled Egg on Toast	6d.
Poached „ „ „	5d.
Welsh Rarebit	6d.
Buck „	9d.
Boiled Egg (local new laid)	3d.
Sardines on Toast ...	6d.
Baked Beans on Toast	5d.
Bacon and Egg	7d.
Ham and Tongue ...	1/-
Cold Ham	8d.
Salmon and Cucumber	8d.
Green Salad	4d.

ICES

Vanilla ... ... 2d. and 4d.	
„ with Cream ...	6d.
Mixed Fruit Sundæ ...	6d.
Grape Fruit Sundæ ...	6d.
Banana and Nut Sundæ	6d.
Milk and Ice Cream ...	4d.
Horlicks and Ice Cream	4d.

Boons and Lings, Laindon High Road.

Above: Vange shops in the 1950s, before the development. (Copyright Essex Record Office)

Opposite: Menu of Enefers Cafe – note the prices.

was complaining of stomach pains. My husband examined her then looked at the mother and said 'It's not surprising that your daughter has pains, she's having a baby.' The mother nearly passed out. My husband had to rush to find a phone, and call an ambulance, which could not get up the road because of the mud and so they had to carry the girl on a stretcher to the main road with my husband walking by her side.

The practice moved to a surgery in Danacre, then when the Laindon Health Centre was built they formed one large practice with Dr Martin and partners.

Janet Millwood

A Land of Milk and Honey

During the 1940s we settled in and like everyone else, we became self-sufficient. We kept chickens, ducks and goats and dad shot rabbits to order, grew vegetables and had seven hives of bees.

Our two goats were kidded in alternate years and when they were in full milk they gave twelve pints a day. The nanny kids were sold in Wickford Market but the Billy goats were slaughtered by Mr Skelton the butcher at Horndon-on-the-Hill who kept the meat for us in his cold store. Spare fruit and vegetables were bottled or made into jam or preserves.

Elsie Hill (*née* Neville)

Victoria Road

My parents came down here in the early days from Bermondsley in about 1920 and bought a plotlands property in Victoria Road and then eventually moved to Worthing Road. My dad was a trade union organiser. He worked in an office in Langdon Road. Mum stayed at home and looked after the children. We had a gas stove and gas lighting and also an Elsen toilet, the contents of which we buried in the garden. My dad grew lovely tomatoes.

Olive Remmington

Above: Shops in Laindon High Road: Charsley's Shoes, Welcome Cafe, Simmonds corn chandlers.

Right: Maud Sergeant and her sister Edna with her parents Maud and John.

Opposite: Hiawatha House before the Second World War.

Weekenders

Just after the Second World War George and I married but we could not get on any council housing list because we were told that we had enough square cubic feet of air. There were four of us, we had two children by this time. In the end we managed to buy a relation's bungalow on a plot of land in Bridge Avenue called the Roost which was near where Tesco's is today. It cost £250 with rates of £5 a year.

We had a single-decker bus in our garden, on land originally owned by someone else who had stopped coming down from London. Mrs Payne, my aunt, just absorbed their land into her garden which was common practice in the

Above: The Laindon Perfumerie, c.1920.

Opposite: Modley's sweet shop in the background at the Fortune of War.

area. On the other side of us the land was owned by an East End couple who spent a lot of time on it. They called the back of our bungalow an 'outerhouse'.

The woman from whom we bought the Roost sold paraffin, eggs and vegetables and when she moved, the weekenders had nowhere to buy paraffin and as we had all the equipment we decided to do it or else they had to walk to the Lower Dunton Road. They used the oil to cook on their little stoves. We were lucky as we had gas for cooking and lighting but the mantels for the lighting were so delicate that if you touched them they disintegrated. We had no electricity, sewerage or water. We originally only had rainwater collected from the roof and piped into a big tank and then they put in a standpipe at the bottom of the road which froze in the winter and we used to put lighted straw round it to thaw it out. I used to take a twenty gallon tank on a wheelbarrow down to the bottom of

the road and push it back up the hill. At the front gate there was an awkward turn and often I would tip the whole lot on the ground and have to go back.

After September the roads were impassable and so we used to order our ration of coal before then. Whifes, the milkman, used to come up here with his little horse and cart to get over the ruts but not every day.

When people did not use a plot for some time somebody commandeered it and when I worked for the Basildon Corporation in the legal department we had great difficulties establishing ownership of some pieces of land.

Maud Sargeant

A Tale of Two Extremes

In 1927 I was born in Bow, East London, in the same house that my mother was born in, forty-one years before. My father was a countryman

who was born in Wickford at the end of the nineteenth-century. He left school at twelve years old and in 1914 joined the Metropolitan Police just as the First World War started and was stationed at Bow and Limehouse. He and my mother married in 1919 and to get away from the pressure of his job he decided one day to buy a four acre field on the Old Hill Estate for £250.

During most of my childhood I had two homes, one in London and the other in Laindon. Dad's land was bordered by ground owned by Mr Brooks on which he kept pigs. The land is now known as The Park and commands wonderful views of the river Thames. On clear nights you can still see the lights on Southend Pier.

At first we had a small white wooden hut, which had built in double beds and a drop-down table. Under the beds we stored bell tents and camp beds which doubled up as dining room benches. We had a sink and draining board plus

a shelf on which we kept our water container and a stove, which, with the Valor paraffin heater, warmed the hut. For lighting we had paraffin and hurricane lamps. We obtained water from a spring-fed pond which was some distance away and shared with four resident families and weekenders.

Elsie Hill (*née* Neville)

Groom/Gardener

My great-great-grandfather came down to Laindon in the 1880s from Boxted as a groom/gardener for the rector Beaumaurice-Stacey Clarke. The Rector held an appointment for Laindon and as he earned seventeen shillings a week he was considered by the locals as a gentleman.

Ken Porter

Above: Working together following a deluge during the 1950s.

Opposite: Ministry of Labour, High Street, Laindon.

Washday

Washday took the whole day and sometimes two. The bathroom was a lean-to built on to the shed and in it was a copper which had to be filled with rain water and the fire lit. The washing was put in the copper and boiled before being put through the mangle, rinsed and then put through again. When the washing was finished the water had to be emptied but dad had built an unofficial drain so we emptied the water into the bath outside the kitchen water outlet which had a bucket with a hole in it, covering the unofficial drain. This was passed, or went unnoticed by the health inspectors.

Drying the clothes during the winter was a problem as we had to dry them in front of the living room fire, forcing us to move into the other room. After the washing dried we ironed it by heating a flat iron on the fire or gas stove. The important thing about heating it was to wipe it or you got your clothes dirty.

Elsie Hill (*née* Neville)

Nests of Adders

The grass used to be high on the railway bank and so there were always nests of adders. One day we went out into the garden and there was an adder sunning himself in our vegetable patch. We did not take any notice as it was all part of the countryside. Provided you did not tread on them they were fine. We had loads of fruit trees – greengages, Victoria plums, apples and grew our own vegetables. The man over the back to us, Mr Legge, used to come down occasionally from London and when he did he would cut the grass and stack it up in great haystacks. The rats used to get in there and then would come into our garden and feed on the chicken food.

Maud Sargeant

Building a Plotland Community

Often our friends from Bow would come down with us and we would erect the bell tents to accommodate them. Some liked it so much that

they bought plots and properties of their own thus forming communities. About 1934 water, which had previously been laid on to the first five properties, was laid along the rest of Old Hill Avenue but not in the side roads where three locked stand pipes were erected. Keys to these were not issued until the water rate was paid. It was an offence to lend somebody your key or leave the tap unlocked. Not long after the Gas Board laid on gas. Some people, with water, installed cesspit drainage, which was emptied by the council in summer and by the residents in winter but the smell was terrible.

The residents and weekenders collected money and built paths along the main avenue. It was an unwritten law that nobody turned out their lights at night until everybody returning from work had passed.

Local tradesmen started delivering goods three times a week and the residents would buy goods for the weekenders, thus saving them the long haul from the shops.

In 1934 we had a brick bungalow built which was the last one on The Old Hill Estate before the law came in forbidding building on Green Belt.

Elsie Hill (*née* Neville)

Village Life

Pitsea in the 1930s would come under the heading of village life. It was a happy period with many hardships. We were short of money but as all the neighbours were in the same position we made the best of things. Some people today would call Pitsea in those days, a shanty town, and once you left the main road with their brick houses you found that most of the dwellings in the side roads were timber framed, lined with asbestos. There was no sanitation and many had chemical closets. Water was obtained from a well supplied from rainwater off the roof through a charcoal filter.

Quite a number of men worked in London and would get a workman's ticket, which would

Tom White relaxing in his garden.

The Professions

In Laindon there were most professions from solicitors, land agents, police and doctors. In St Nicholas Lane you could register a death or birth. Laindon even had its own telephone and labour exchange.

Elsie Hill (*née* Neville)

Mud Tracks

Orsett Hospital used to empty the ashes from their boilers every so often and our men would go down and collect it on a Sunday to lay on the roads but it was difficult without a car. A couple used to have a car and used to bring some back. People would hammer tins flat and lay them in the ruts. I remember my young son Peter, walking through the ice filled ruts in his wellington boots.

The kids' idea of a good time was to go up to the railway bridge and look over at the trains below.

Maud Sargeant

Northlands

In 1916 my grandparents bought a farm in Northlands when my father was five. They had large families in those days and he was the youngest of thirteen children. When he left school he went to work on the farm and looked after the animals.

Margaret Browning

Born in Whitechapel Hospital

My grandfather worked in the London Hospital Whitechapel as a fitter and decided that the only place that was good enough for his daughter to have his grandchild was that hospital. Mum and gran were shopping in Pitsea Market on a Wednesday when mum said she had a bit of a tummy ache. My grandmother shook her head and said 'You've been eating too many boiled

cost one shilling and four pence return provided they arrived in Fenchurch Street before 8 a.m. I remember the lovely fresh air that greeted me as I got out at Pitsea station, after a hot stuffy day in London.

Red-letter days were Wednesdays and Saturdays, market days, when neighbours met and exchanged gossip and we enjoyed a couple of hours just looking around. You could buy many things for a few pence and many items were second hand.

Summer evenings and weekends were spent in the garden where we grew vegetables and flowers which helped with the low wages we earned. Sometimes we would go for a walk and would see robins, blue-tits, chaffinches and cuckoos. There were rabbits that one could catch on Pitsea Marshes. On one occasion an adder crossed the path and I killed it with a spade and when I looked closer I realized it was in the act of swallowing a toad.

The late Tom White

ENEFERS CAFE & BAKERY
SOUTHEND ARTERIAL ROAD
FORTUNE OF WAR ROUNDABOUT
Half-way stop for coaches.
Service or Private.

Tel :
LAINDON
2329

MAKE
THIS
YOUR
ROAD
STOP

Enefers business card –
note the telephone number.

sweets,' but it was not, it was me on the way. Mum went by ambulance all the way from Pitsea to Whitechapel.

Sandra Bonnett (née Keyes)

Charlie the Chimney Sweep

Charlie Sewell the chimney sweep would buy boxes of sweets to sell on. We would go to his bungalow clutching our half-pence for sweets and then sit on the doorstep watching the black-birds in the apple trees and the bees flying into the observation hive.

Elsie Hill (née Neville)

We thought we had Ghosts

We lived above Norton's shop and used all the rooms except one which Nortons used as a furniture store. Early one Sunday morning mum appeared white as a sheet 'There's noises in there,' pointing to the room. 'What shall we do?' Dad was in the Merchant Navy and there was nobody around.

The noise went on all day and into the night. Next morning, Mr Norton came in and mum told him. He looked surprised and said 'It can't be, there's nobody in there.' Slowly he opened the door and looked round the room and then smiled as two jackdaws stared back at him. They must have come down the chimney.

Margaret Browning

Nothing was Locked Up

We would cycle down to the station and leave our bikes in the bike shed outside, nobody touched them and I would also go out and leave the bungalow unlocked. People were so honest.

Maud Sargeant

Six Rabbits in a Pot

My mother would put six rabbits in a saucepan which hung by a chain over a big old log fire. Then she would put in dumplings, carrots and turnips and that would feed the family.

Fred Broom

Robinson's Dolls' Hospital, 1920s.

Shops at Pitsea

There were over ninety shops in Pitsea and on the High Road, there was Norton's the furniture shop, a greengrocers, the bank on the corner, a coal yard and on the front there were hoardings which advertised the cinema. The post office sorting office was a little hut. My cousin had a florists shop and when she moved out they converted it to a post office. There was a butchers, fish shop, a boot shop and a shop where Howards collected their rents.

We had everything really and when the new town people first moved in they used to come to Pitsea for their shopping. There was a departmental store which had a system where when you had made a purchase they put the money into a tube which was sent up to the office and came back with your change and a receipt.

Margaret Browning

Cycling Down to Laindon

I used to cycle to the shops in Laindon High Road to get the shopping for my parents and between the station and the Fortune of War there were at least 100 shops. I would go to Sizers the butchers, Finch's the greengrocers, Slopes' dairy and Boon's newsagents. In Laindon you could buy anything from furniture to chicken feed.

John Rugg

Laindon Hotel, 1930s.

Giving Birth

I had both our children in Billericay Hospital, which was an old workhouse. At that time Basildon Hospital had not been built. With one of my children I was in the early stages of labour and walked down to the town centre through the muddy lanes with the intention of catching a bus to Billericay but in the end I had to call an ambulance. In those days there was one particular midwife who was horrible to any unmarried mother. The hospital would only allow husbands to visit and nobody else, so unmarried mothers had no visitors. One woman's husband was working in Cornwall and could not visit her. This midwife said to her 'You are either not married or your husband cannot be bothered to see you.' You can imagine how she felt.

In those days they would not let you out of the hospital until your baby was five pounds. As my son had not reached that weight they kept me in for three weeks, continually feeding him.

The late Yvonne Smith (*née* Brasier)

My Children were Born at Home

I had my baby at home and had to manage by boiling water from the well. The two doctor's surgeries in Laindon were lovely. There was one on the corner of St Nicholas Lane, where the housing office is now and the other was in Hiawatha in the High Road.

Olive Remmington

High Street, Laindon.

The Colony

People from the East End who had no work came down here to this wonderful house and grounds. The gardens were laid out like an Elizabethan garden with lots and lots of pathways and fruit trees. They had pigs and the kids used to love to feed them. A farmer called Gray bought it and laid it out as a caravan park.

Maud Sargeant

Winters

Winters could be tough, we would wake on cold mornings to find fern-like patterns inscribed on the inside of the bedroom windows but the unmade roads with the endless ruts of sticky, muddy clay were our biggest challenge. It was said if you lived in Pitsea you were born with webbed feet.

Margaret Jackson

two

Impending Change

We knew they were going to Develop

As young children we knew that the area was going to be developed and gradually our friends' parents sold up and moved to different parts of the country. Many were frightened of the future. Some of the owners were pleased to sell to the corporation and move into a brand new house but others hated the loss of their way of life

The corporation bought both our parents' properties but as second generation we were not entitled to housing. If you were a second generation council tenant or you came down from London and obtained a job as a key worker, you were re-housed.

When we first got married we had a small place in Leicester Road on which they later built Blue House Community Centre. We had a bucket-and-chuck-it toilet and were concerned when we had our first baby because we got our water from a well but Dr Long reassured us by saying if it had newts in it the water was safe. When we moved into the two-bedroomed flat above Parkinson's shop we thought we were in heaven because it had a proper toilet and running cold water.

As kids we played football, cricket and hop-scotch in the street as there were very few cars to stop us. The only vehicles that stopped our games were the horses and carts of Cottis, the baker and the milkman.

Olive Remmington

Beginning of the End

One after another, people left the area and sold to the corporation especially the weekenders. One lady who lived in a Nissan hut sold, which was quickly followed by one old man who was like a farmer. Gradually all the footpaths became overgrown and brambles clawed at you as you passed making getting about very difficult. With the plotlands dying it got lonely so finally we decided to sell.

Maud Sargeant

They Started Buying Properties

Basildon Corporation started buying up property and my uncle, who was a councillor in Pitsea saw what was happening but nobody took any notice of him and so in the end he moved out of the area.

David Pratt

Laindon during the 1920s before the development.

A. W. COLEMAN & CO.

SOLICITORS.
COMMISSIONERS FOR OATHS.

H. G. ASPLIN.   G. T. MEPHAM
S. A. JEWERS.   J. M. CHANNER
C. R. GLENNY.   H. J. T. JEWERS
J. AFFLECK

R. B. ASPLIN (AND IN AUSTRALIA)

AND AT BANK CHAMBERS, LONDON ROAD, PITSEA
AND CHURCH HOUSE, 46, HIGH STREET, BILLERICAY
ALSO AS HATTEN, ASPLIN, JEWERS & GLENNY.
GRAYS AND BARKING.

Telephone- LAINDON 2107.

15, HIGH STREET.
LAINDON,
ESSEX.

12th. April, 1960.
Our ref:- WDW/JM.

Mrs. G.E. Pratt,
Enifers Cafe,
Arterial Road,
Laindon.

Dear Madam,

re:- Yourself and the Corporation.

We are pleased to inform you that your sale to the Corporation has now been Completed. We therefore enclose herewith our cheque for £10.0.0., and return the Title Deeds and Documents.

Yours faithfully,

A letter from a solicitor acknowledging the sale of a piece of land to the Basildon Development Corporation.

Where the Town Started

I was born in Chadwell Heath and went to Canvey Island during the war to live with my aunt. Eventually my family moved to Sandon Road Pitsea which is where the new town started.

Horace Remmington

The Road was Punctuated by Gaps

When you walked down the road in Pitsea it was punctuated with gaps where people had moved out or had not taken up occupation.

Margaret Jackson

The New Houses were Not for Us

My mother sold her place to Basildon Development Corporation in 1963 as they were buying up properties and they did help her to find a plot in Berry Lane. In 1965 we got married and applied to the corporation for housing but as we lived in Southminster they refused us and said we did not qualify because they were only offering properties to people from London.

Ken Porter

They Bought our Bungalow for £750

My parents had a bungalow called Lingdale in Edgware Drive where Knights is now. We had three plots of land extending to Brentford Avenue. Being only track roads they were extremely muddy in winter. We had no drains, no electricity but did have gas and dad eventually got the water put on to save using the well.

One evening dad went to a meeting where an MP spoke and the Basildon Development Corporation gave out books and maps advising everybody what was likely to happen. When dad came home from the meeting he did not seem too worried and said 'We live in mud and all that

Pitsea Service Station in the early 1950s before the development. (Copyright Essex Record Office)

Day by Day

I can remember walking to Laindon Station from Pound Lane, along St Nicholas Lane and the High Road to catch the train for work. At first there were fields and then gradually day by day it changed. First they built the roads and then the houses and over the years it changed dramatically.

John Rugg

will happen is there will be more mud.'
He got upset when he realized that Basildon Development Corporation would not be rehousing us in a modern house. As this became general knowledge it panicked people into moving. The Basildon Development Corporation purchased our bungalow for £750 which was not enough to buy another property in Kings Road so dad had to take out a long term loan from his firm in London. The week after we moved out they knocked the bungalow down.

Ann Rugg (*née* Bullimore)

The Town gradually Grew

When we came down here I mainly shopped in Laindon, which had a great variety of shops. In the town was the Co-op. Alf Dove, the councillor, was the manager. The town was gradually growing and East Walk had just opened.

Janet Millwood

Our Road has not Changed Much

My wife and I moved to Elm Tree Road Pitsea in the 1960s and apart from the council building the road at the bottom nothing has changed much despite the Basildon Development Corporation taking over.

Tony Read

We Could Not Sell

We bought a one-bedroomed bungalow on the Primrose Estate. It had a dining room and a kitchen. We had our two children in it but it became too small for our growing family and so we decided to sell. The girl in Temple Mead Estate Agents said we would easily sell it. Somebody came to buy it and then the district valuer advised us that we could only sell to the Basildon Development Corporation as they were buying up all the land to build the new town. We originally paid £400 for it and I thought that I should sell it for the same. The district valuer offered £550 and then a new law came in and we received £600. With that money we put a deposit on a house in Upminster which was being sold for £1,700. Then we decided against it for although it would have saved us money travelling up to London each day we decided to

Clayhill Road during the 1960s. (Copyright Basildon Council)

Ted Lawrence in 1969 at Lodge Stores, Markhams Chase, now the Community Hall.

accept a property from Basildon Development Corporation in Falkenham Rise. The houses were built by French the builders and were good buildings. We stayed there for a year and then we managed to buy our present property. We did not have a lot but we had enough food and were very happy.

The late Yvonne Smith

Some Emigrated

The building of the new town did what the war did not. It scattered the original residents of the area across the world. Very few took up the offer of rented accommodation and chose to move out to other parts of the country, some emigrated to Australia and Canada.

Margaret Jackson

Laindon Link

I remember in the 1950s when they started building Basildon especially the construction of Laindon Link. Giant earthmovers moved in, tearing down trees and cutting out the roadway. I had just started school and was going to what

is now known as Janet Dukes School, but then known as Markhams Chase Primary. My brother Barry, Martin Hale from next door, Jimmy Nicholls, Godfrey Hope, David Townsend and I used to play soldiers amongst the great mounds of earth thrown up by the machinery. The Link was started next to the public conveniences opposite Somerset Road. On one side used to be Parkinson's Garage and on the other was Charles Markham's dairy and shop.

Brian Baylis

Up to our Waists in Water

When we lived in Rectory Road my husband and I used to walk along the pathway at the back to the Winged Horse which had a great ditch running along both sides. Then one night, in 1953, we went to the Winged Horse and I was wearing sandals and a cotton yellow skirt.

While we were having a drink somebody came in, shook their umbrella, and said, 'It's belting down out there.' A man rang for a taxi but was told they had all been cancelled because of the floods. It was pouring down when we stepped out of the pub and we had to make

Lee Chapel North, 1950.

The late Yvonne Smith at the time of interview.

our way along the footpath up to our waists in cold water. When we got home the water was just oozing through the floor boards and we decided that if things got worse we would go up into the roof space. Then we had an ARP man knock on the door to make sure we were all right.

Margaret Browning

Tyler Avenue

I entered this world Sunday 8 September 1946 in No. 6, Tyler Avenue Laindon, my mum being Sybil, and dad, Frank Baylis. Tyler Avenue in

those days was mainly rubble. Sadly, the house has since been demolished and a car park now stands where the back garden was.

Brian Baylis

Compulsory Purchase

When the corporation started taking over there was not enough resistance. People did not realize what was happening. Once owners were served with a compulsory purchase order they started getting indignant but it was too late. I remember when our letter came through we were hopping mad. All they offered was £750 for my parents'

Brian Baylis' parents on a day trip.

New Arterial Road before development,
late 1920s.

property in Cambridge Road. We went to a solicitor and we found out they could do it. Mum bought a place near Webster's pig farm, which was run down but we managed to get it sorted out.

We bought some building plots and the corporation took half of them for £10 and then sent us the bill for fencing.

David Pratt

Laindon's Shops Shrivelled and Died

I started in politics because I did not like what was happening to Laindon. When we first moved here my wife used to walk down a pathway, (Durham Road) that had a concrete path just the width of pram wheels. Victoria Road went right through to Lower Dunton Road and the whole of the High Street, through to the station consisted of shops that had everything. Slowly they were driven out and many moved to the town centre and Laindon started to shrivel and die. I felt it was wrong and so I got involved and fought for better compensation for the owners, for better jobs and roads.

Vic York

Laindon during the 1930s.

Thoughts Of New Laindon

The scene was once so very different trees and grass where now is stone,
great concrete jungles flourish upon the fields we used to roam.
Small wooden buildings painted gaily, a thicket hedge enclosing all,
wobbly gates with creaking hinges these things are now beyond recall.
Where are the lanes we used to wander? Where are the fields so lush and green, struck down
beneath that sword called progress, it so sharp its cut is clean.
Gone favourite haunts of childhood, sunlit meadows, hill and dells.
Gone the stillness of the country now traffic drowns the old church bells.
One generation cries in protest against the things the next will do but time goes marching
onwards with scant respect for me or you.

Betty Morley (*née* Ives)

three

Preparing
for Life

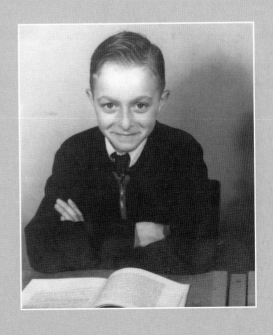

A Class of Eighty

The area was well served with schools and the village school in Laindon High Road was built in 1860. In the 1920s and 1930s the main schools were Laindon Hills, Markhams Chase, Dunton, and Laindon Park. The latter was known as Donaldson's.

In 1934 there was a re-organisation of schools and during the war, with the influx of children coming down from London because of the blitz, schools became overcrowded. At one time, just for a short period, there was a class of eighty.

Elsie Hill (*née* Neville)

Ponds School, Dunton

The first school I went to was a house on Dunton plotlands which had only seven pupils, five girls and two boys, one of them was the vicar's son. We had our lessons in one room and our teacher, Mrs Dobins, used to cook our dinners on a range cooker. She used to teach us everything and we wrote on slates as there was no blackboard. She would write on the top of our slates in chalk and we would copy it. There was no real playground and we used to play in the orchard. We played hee, hop scotch, five stones and in the autumn, conkers.

When I went to Laindon Hills School it seemed so big with over 100 pupils but it did me good because I learnt to mix. We moved round from class room to class room, having different lessons with different teachers.

Maureen Read

Tractor Driving

When I was a kid I used to spend my spare time working at Colvile Farm which is where Basildon Hospital is now. I helped with the harvest, cut the grass, and helped out with the animals. One day, when I was about fourteen I was driving the tractor back after cutting some grass and was taking the big roundabout near the town centre when a copper stepped out and stopped me. I thought this is it as it was illegal for me to drive but he held the traffic up and waved me round.

David Pratt

Charlie Markham's Dairy

Whilst at college between 1945 and 1947 we had to do a project on a local industry and I chose to go to Charlie Markham's dairy which was in Laindon High Road. Milk was brought in churns from local farms, bottled and was delivered the same day. Occasionally the milk was brought round in churns and people came out with jugs which the milkman filled. Charlie said that he wished people would not wash out their bottles as you could not tell what they had put in them. The coalman also made his deliveries by horse and cart.

Elsie Hill (*née* Neville)

Laindon Hills

We got our three children into the excellent Laindon Hills School. One of the teachers Miss Wilkins used to play the piano accordion for country dancing. One of the local boys, who went to Dunton School, said to me that I ought to let my three go to his school as all they did was to play with mud pies. When we moved to Great Gregorie Peter and Pat went to Woodlands and Janet won a scholarship and went to Barnstable.

Janet my daughter loved physical training, she took after my husband George.

Maud Sargeant

Headmistress

When I opened Ryedene Primary School in Vange in 1979 I noticed the school field was covered in broken glass and rubbish, so I arranged for the children to clear it. About

Laindon Hills School, 1903. The Headmistress Miss Howlett is on the left. Teacher Miss Roper is on the right.

a fortnight later we had a very heavy storm and I looked out on the field and was surprised to see that it was again littered with rubbish. Suddenly, I realised what had caused it. The field had been two roads and all the rubbish from that part of the plotlands had been buried, bashed or burned over the years and the heavy rain had exposed it.

Elsie Hill (*née* Neville)

A Special Teacher

I went to school at Markhams Chase, now called Janet Dukes which was in walking distance of Pound Lane. School never interested me unless it was sport. The head mistress was Mrs Duke but the teacher that influenced me most was Mr Wallace who was a very strong disciplinarian but a good teacher. At that time you had a fear of adults. On one occasion there was a small kid called Billy who was playing Mr Wallace up and so he pulled down his socks and gave him a real good slapping. That really registered. We liked our music teacher, Miss Cook.

In the last year at the school Mr Devrne showed me how to hold a bat and bowl. He was also responsible for my faith. He used to tell us biblical stories which stimulated our imaginations. At the end of the day he would ask 'What do you want to do now?' and we would reply 'A story.' He would then pull the blackboard down on which was a map of Israel and he would tell us a biblical story.

Ken Porter

School Secretary

We both went to Markhams Chase School (now Janet Duke's) although my husband is three years older than me. His mother worked in the school

Vange School, early 1960s. (Copyright Essex Record Office)

as the school secretary for more than thirteen years.

Ann Rugg (*née* Bullimore)

Getting the Cane

My mother went to Pitsea School and I followed in her footsteps just before the war. I was left handed and every time I tried to write with my left hand they rapped me over the knuckles with a thick red pencil. I loved knitting but because I was left handed the school would not teach me. When I went to Craylands I got the cane for talking.

Margaret Browning

'Oscar' at Pitsea School

In 1957 I took my eleven-plus at Pitsea School where three-quarters of my class passed. I think it was the teachers who were responsible for the good results. It was the best school in the area and everybody wanted to go there, although St Margaret's was a very good school and a lot of business people sent their children there.

I remember some of the teachers, Mr Jones was the Head until the 1980s. There was Miss Witt and Mr Green, who was a bit of a disciplinarian. He had a slipper called Oscar, and if the boys did anything wrong, they got the slipper and the girls got a slap round the legs. I got a slap once when my capitals touched the top of the page. It did not do us any harm.

I decided to go to Palmers girls' grammar school in Grays because I liked the colour of the uniform, which was a cornflower blue. I could have gone to Fryerns as it was the first year they opened their doors. Most of the class went there but a few girls went to Southend. We had bus passes and went on Eastern National to One Tree Hill and then picked up a school bus from there.

Sandra Bonnett (*née* Keyes)

Pitsea School

In the last year of the junior school I remember Mr Bebbington holding handwriting competitions. You could challenge anyone in the league above and if your work was considered better you changed places with them. He was particular about clean shoes – a real challenge for those who lived in unmade roads.

Margaret Jackson

Guitar Player

Gary, my grandson, has played at the Cavern Club in Liverpool with the group Colour Kinesis, and is touring in the Manchester area.

Joy Ayres

Helping with the Harvest

School used to give us three weeks off to help with the harvest then they gave me another eight weeks and I never went back because I had turned fourteen. In those days, during the war, anybody who worked on the farm was exempt during harvest time.

Fred Broom

Lee Chapel South School

Jonathan, my son, went to Lee Chapel South School which had a good name. I used to drop him off on my way to work. My son went to Barnstable after that and became a photographer and photographed the dismantling of one of Sellafield's reactors but is now teaching. His wife went into the ministry.

My daughter went to Kingswood. I remember the head mistress, Mrs Fox, who was an excellent headmistress.

Janet Millwood

Walked for Miles

As a child on the plotlands I would walk for miles with my dog and would read and read anything and everything by the gas light. There was no library but I would borrow books for two pence a week from a shop in the High Street. Later there was a travelling library.

The late Yvonne Smith (*née* Brasier)

Markhams Chase School

Markhams Chase School was built in 1931 and the headmistress, Janet Duke used to get upset because some children had no shoes. One day all the kids ran after the chain grass cutter and she was worried because she thought that they might get hurt. Next morning at assembly she lined up the thirty guilty children and caned them.

During the war there were no male teachers as they had all been called up. I can remember some of the teachers names as if it were yesterday, Miss McMillan, Miss O'Dell and Miss Mears. I failed my eleven-plus and went to Laindon High Road but took it again at thirteen and passed. I then went to Mid-Essex Technical College at Chelmsford.

Roy Ives

Across the Stile to School

When I first started going to Markhams Chase School I used to cut through Bluehouse Farm and then when Laindon Link opened I used that. Later they fenced off what was left of Bluehouse Farm but we still used the stile although the land was a quagmire.

Brian Baylis

Corporal Punishment

I went to a mixed school at Laindon Park (Donaldson's School). They were very strict and the boys would get the cane for anything. One teacher always seemed in a bad temper to us

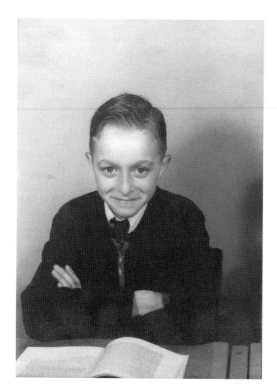

Brian Baylis at school in the 1950s.

Fivestones

We lived in Brackendale Road which had a lot of professional people who frowned on kids playing in the street and so I used to go over to my cousins at Pitsea to play. We played five-stones, Mr Wolf and we were always out on our bikes. It was wonderful, you could wander anywhere in safety.

Sandra Bonnett (*née* Keyes)

Eleven-Plus

I went to Markhams Chase School, which later became Janet Dukes. The headmistress must have been good as they named the school after her. I remember one of the teachers, Miss Whitley. I then went to Laindon High Road School for two years and then after sitting the examination at thirteen went to Chelmsford Technical School. I had to start out early to get to school as I had to catch two buses. My father used to help me with my home work and was keen that we got a good education.

Olive Remmington

kids, he hit one kid round the head so hard that it hit the desk.

The teachers I remember were Mrs Pritchard who took general subjects and our PE teacher Mrs Jollymans. I found that in a 'B' class I could keep up but not in an 'A'.

Thelma Broom

four

They Came
From All
Corners

The Birth of a New Town

In the fifties you could climb up the bank at Laindon, look across and see the town gradually taking shape.

Maud Sargeant

Nottingham

In 1964 Bob my husband worked for York Shipley in Nottingham and one day, Bob came home and declared that the firm was moving to Basildon New Town and that if he went we would be allocated a new, two-bedroomed house.

About thirty volunteered to go and for two months they travelled down to Basildon all week, coming home on Friday night. After what seemed ages we received a letter from Basildon Development Corporation offering us a new house in St Nicholas Lane. Bob watched it go up brick by brick. Then, we got another letter telling us that the house was finished. York Shipley arranged our removals and we were given money to help with the expenses.

Janet Garrard

Paddington

I was born in Paddington and when I was four we moved to Church Road, Laindon to an asbestos bungalow called Bellview but nobody used to worry about asbestos in those days. Later it was replaced with brick.

Thelma Broom

Durham

I was born in 1939 at Horden in County Durham, a mining village. At one time it was the deepest deep mine in the country. We were all right but some kids went to school barefoot and with the backside hanging out of their trousers. Most of the miners were out most nights and weekends getting drunk.

I was the first paper boy in Peterlee and used to help out by putting my money in the family pot but one day mum and dad paid me back by buying me a bike for twenty-one pounds, which was a lot of money in those days. I have three sisters and two brothers.

I started work as an apprentice carpenter and joiner with a joinery company and then worked for the National Coal Board. The very first thing I made was a pair of steps which I have still got. Gradually I worked my way up to the drawing office and then to general foreman and then back in the mining subsidence office. It was the most interesting job I've ever had. About this time I got married and looked around for a job with more money. I took a job as a production manager and then became an estimator.

I then saw a position advertised for a maintenance surveyor with Basildon Development Corporation. I got the job and was put in Eddie Boxall's void property section. He was responsible for inspecting empty properties and preparing them for letting throughout the new town. I was based at the Hatherly Office. I was promoted to area surveyor at Fryerns and then at Pitsea and finished up in charge of capital works. When we came here we were allocated a three-bedroomed house at Newberry Side on the Five Links Estate. The house looked out on to a square which was all right once you shut your front door, but the garden was very small.

Jim Turnbull

Forest Gate

I was born in the hospital at Forest Gate and was the youngest of six and lived in Oakdale Road in a two-up two-down house. We had the upstairs and so we were a bit cramped.

When John, my husband, came up for his interview with Basildon Development Corporation in 1956 I looked out of the top window of our place in Leyton waiting for him. Then I saw him coming along the road and when I saw

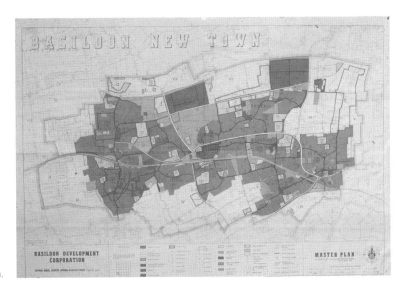

Plan of Basildon.

his face I thought 'He's not got the job.' I was wrong and for two weeks John had to travel to Basildon before we were allocated our house. We were lucky, they gave us a choice of a three-bedroomed house for two pounds one shilling and eight pence or a two-bedroomed for one pound eighteen shilling and nine pence. We chose the cheaper property but it was lovely having our own front door.

We wanted a television and so we cashed in an insurance policy and used it for a deposit on one but we had to go to Radio Rentals in Westcliff as there were no television shops in Basildon. For our normal shopping we had to walk to Pitsea pushing a pram which was laden on the way back.

We missed our family in London but like most families at that time we did not have a car and so when we went up to see them we had to catch the X10 bus which went right to Victoria. It would be late when we got home and we would have to walk up Whitmore Way in the pitch black. At first I hated living in Basildon and like a lot of young women I was homesick.

Pat Radley

A Cockney from Bow

I was born in 1930 in Bow which makes me a cockney. Mum and dad had a little place in Palm Street and we were very lucky because we moved to Leytonstone just before the war and a landmine landed on our old house flattening it.

My dad was a lighterman and worked on the barges which carried timber. People were hard up in those days but were wonderful. I had four sisters, Rosie, Dolly, Ada and Kitty. To make food go round mum made lots of stews.

One day my mate and I went fishing in the canal with a little net. We were enjoying ourselves so much that we forgot the time and did not get home till dark. We were really in trouble as mum had the whole street out looking for us. People were so honest and would leave their doors open or leave their keys on a piece of string just inside the letter box.

I went to Bancroft Road School where we were given half-a-bottle of milk and in the afternoon, made to sleep.

I left school in 1944 aged fourteen and started work in the Co-op. I used to travel on my bike collecting rents. One day, Mr Quirk, the estate manager, called me into the office and told me to change my cockney accent.

The Co-op let flats over shops and when I got married in 1954 I asked for one of these, but they allocated it to a chemist, I was so annoyed I applied for a job with Basildon Development Corporation because a house went with it and was allocated a two-bedroomed house in Trimley Close.

John Radley

Leicestershire

I was born in Leicestershire in 1928 and went to school there but when I was seventeen we moved to Sudbury's Farm in Little Burstead where my father started work. We lived in a little place by the side of the road just before the farm. There was no sanitation and we had to do it in a bucket, in a shed round the back. We had an old stove and a primus stove to cook on and oil lamps for lighting.

In 1948 Keelings, the farm people got us this council house in Pound Lane. You had to work on the land to get one.

Fred Broom

Bermondsey

I was born in Bermondsey in 1926 and went to St Saviours's and St Olive's Grammar School for girls. Most students paid but I had won a scholarship. In 1939 the war broke out and my sister and I were evacuated to Hove. We were put with a very high-class family who lived in a three-storey mansion. In the afternoon the ladies from the area came for tea and the cook would make them malt bread. Mother was not allowed to come and see us. We were so unhappy that my sister wrote mum a letter, cried on it and rubbed in the tears to smudge it. It did the trick and she came down and took us home. There was no school for me to go to and I had lost my scholarship because I came home. As I was fourteen and could leave school, I went to work for a florists. I worked seven days a week for

eleven shilling and six pence and used to make wreaths and bouquets for funerals and weddings. Each day I travelled up to Spitalfields Market with the boss to purchase flowers and on the way back I used to jump up on the lorry and open the wooden boxes to show the local florists the flowers we had for sale. I loved it. As the war was on we could not get new frames for wreaths and so we would go to the cemeteries and pick up old ones with the dead flowers and wires on. I used to pick them over and get them back into use again.

Maud Sargeant

My Old Man said Follow the Van

After a few years of marriage it is surprising how much stuff you accumulate as I found out when I went to make arrangements to move to Basildon. A friend of ours knew this bloke who agreed to move us on his van. We loaded everything on it but there was not enough room so we had to leave our coal behind; then at the last moment my friend asked if we would take his bike and babies' pram. I had to sit on the tailboard and the man shouted back at me 'If you start falling off, bang on the side!' The van was in a terrible state and it puffed along on bald tyres at thirty miles an hour.

John Radley

Charles Caravan Park

In 1959 we bought a caravan in Ilford High Road and brought it down to Charles Caravan Park in Dunton. We were delighted because we had our own front door. A hot water tank was attached to the chimney so that when the fire was alight we had hot water. I turned the end bedroom into a nursery for our daughter Julia. She got to know a lot of people on the site because she used to lean out of her window and say hello to everyone who passed early in the morning. Each day I drove my motorbike

Laindon Hills Estate in the
1970s.

up to Gants Hill and then caught the tube into
London where I was a draughtsman with Castrol
and then on Saturday I worked at Burtons,
which used to pay my fares all week.

Vic York

Wooden Council Offices

Most of the newcomers to Basildon in 1961
were young and trustworthy and overall the area
was much quieter. In those early days the town
centre was sparse with very few shops. Where
the market now stands there were three butchers,
two bakers and a store owned by Littlewoods. In
the square there was a large supermarket who
gave pink stamps with your purchase and where
Halifax bank now stands was Tesco. There was
Chinese restaurant above where Barclays Bank
stands and Primark is where the Co-op once
stood. Woolworth and Sainsbury's stores were
opposite where the fountain is now. Where
Wilkins now stands, once stood the wooden
buildings of the library and council offices.

Roy Wallis

Leyton

In 1962 my mum and dad moved from Leyton
to The Upway. Dad was still working and used to
travel to Temple Mills in Stratford each day.

Pat Radley

We could not get Re-housed

When we got married in 1958 we bought a
piece of land, although we had hardly any money.
At first, we lived with my mother and tried to
rent a property from the council but we did not
qualify, then we tried the Basildon Development
Corporation but it was the same story. Then an
old lady who worked for us at the Enefer cafe
said she had a small bungalow she wanted to sell
and so we saved up and bought it. It was only
an old shack. She did have permission to build
a house on it but by the time we had saved up
enough money the permission had expired and
they would not renew it. About a year later
Basildon Development Corporation wrote to us
and said they wanted half this land to put a water
pipe in and they offered us £10. We were a little
suspicious of solicitors in Laindon so we went to
one in Southend but he told us the same.

Gayle Pratt

The Town Centre was Empty

The town centre had no shops and my sister and
I used to go to Pitsea Market for shopping. At
The Jolly Friar there was the Home & Colonial
and on the corner of Downey Close there was
Howard's Dairy which was a little mobile shop
and sold everything. At that time there was no
railway station in Basildon and no hospital.

Pat Radley

Scenes from Basildon town centre.

Farmer Brown

Where Wykes Green is now there used to be Farmer Brown's where we used to buy our eggs. In the end Basildon Development Corporation compulsorily purchased his land and built Curling Tye and Wykes Green on it.

John Radley

Pitsea Market

On Wednesday and Saturday Pitsea market would throb with people who came from miles around. The stalls were just like old cattle sheds and the stallholders sold everything from second-hand to new. One market trader, Mr Cohen used to throw plates in the air, catch them and ask 'what will you give me for these?' Years ago the Market was in Station Lane and then it moved across the other side of the road.

Horace Remmington

New Town Blues

When we came here in 1958 there was no town centre and we had to go to Pitsea to shop. Most people got on well because we were all in the same boat. We had all moved away from our extended families but a lot of people got the 'new town blues' because of it and could not cope on their own. There were no clubs and nothing to do so some took tranquilizers to help with their depression.

I was lucky because my sister Rene came down first and then mum and dad, followed by my cousin and so gradually the family built up. My sister and I used to go to evening classes at Fryerns' School where she made a book case and I made a coffee table.

Joy Ayres

'Hello Playmates'

One of the first shops that opened in the town centre was John Waltons, which was a gents' outfitters and was opened by the late comedian Arthur – 'Hello Playmates' – Askey. In December 1961, when I was about to leave school, mum and dad took me there and bought me the last outfit they paid for.

Opposite John Waltons was Tesco, which I believe was the first supermarket in Basildon. Another one which opened was Superfare where mum worked. My brother-in-law worked in the gent's hairdressers known as Jeffries. Behind Superfare was Halfords. When I started work I traded in the bike I had bought off my sister for five pounds for a brand new one. Other shops were the newsagents, Martin's or Forbuoys and MacFisheries.

Brian Baylis

Basildon Market

During the sixties we were excited because Basildon Market opened. At first all the market traders had were sheets on the floor but they sold everything. The first shop to open in the town centre was Mayes of Wickford.

Joy Ayres

five

Basildon at Work

Home in Time for Dick Barton

When we first moved to Sudbury Farm in 1945, the farmer at first had cows then changed over to 400 acres of corn. We used to thrash it with an old thrashing machine which ran off a puffing steam engine and made a hell of a noise. I then went to work for Keelings who thrashed most of the corn for the farmers round here and I worked on most of the farms in the area. As a youngster, they occasionally let me steer the steam engines which was great but you really had to be a certain age for that and I wasn't. We got married when I was eighteen and we lived in a little old place called Dairy Cote and I used to cycle to work and had to be there by six in the morning. Old Keeling used to say 'If you're not here at six don't bother to come at all.' When we finished I used to jump on my bike and rush home to be in time to listen to Dick Barton on the radio, about seven.

The main skill you had to have was strength, the sacks weighed over two hundred and a quarter pounds. In those days I could throw one of them across the trailer and think nothing of it. The corn was stacked in the barn. You would feed the corn into the thrashing machine and the straw would land on to a bailer and be tied up and pushed out at the end. A bloke would hook it and run it up a ladder and stack it on the hay stack. They would make a round bit at the top and sometimes put thatch on it. They used the barley straw to feed the cattle and the corn for bedding them down. In the old days most of the farms had cattle and sheep. Years ago I was loading a cart with sacks of corn on Crawfords Farm and the old farmer said 'Can't you get more on top boy?' so I did, and as the wagon pulled away it broke in half.

Fred Broom

Initiation Ceremony

When I left school I did a seven-year apprenticeship as an agricultural engineer at Howards at West Horndon. I earned twenty-five shillings a week out of which I used to give my mum one pound. I went to Southend College one day and one evening a week. I worked from 7.30 a.m. till 6 p.m. After tea I earned extra money by working for Parkinson's Taxis until 1 a.m.

When you started work in those days they had an initiation ceremony where they would blacken certain parts of your body but it did not work with me. I picked up a hammer and said 'The first one that touches me gets this!'

David Pratt

Artist

I attended Southend College for a year with a friend. She wanted to do abstract art. The tutor was really pleased with us and so we decided to go to Sir John Cass College. He set up a college for those people who had not reached their artistic potential and I was there for eight years. I learnt sculpture, brasscasting, painting and silversmithing. I supplied items to Hatton Garden and sold a lot of my sculptures.

The late Yvonne Smith (*née* Brasier)

Dressmaker

I was brought up in Easington Colliery, a mining village and when I left school at fifteen I went to work in a machine factory where I learned men's tailoring. When Jim and I married we lived in a number of houses but the last one was lovely and we bought it. Jim obtained a job in Basildon as a surveyor and we moved down here in the early seventies. There were not many shops in Basildon then. Jim's sister lived round the corner and we started doing homework.

Sadie Turnbull

The Happiest Days of my Life

I ploughed my first field when I was thirteen. Old farmer Sharp used to plough his fields with three horses and one day I was leading a young horse which was being broken in. Suddenly somebody came running across the field and told Farmer Sharp his father had died. He said 'I've got to go, will you finish the field?' He was away for three days and during that time I ploughed three big fields. They were the happiest days of my life.

Fred Broom

Tom Wright supervising the construction of the sculpture.

Pitsea Market

Pitsea Market was wonderful and had some real characters. They would throw plates in the air and catch them. They would start off with the patter 'I'm not asking twenty pounds for this, I am not even asking for ten, for you, you look a good crowd and the fact they have fallen off the back of a lorry you can have it for a fiver!'. There was Alf the market man who sold leather coats and Mrs Ling who sold second-hand goods. Like most people in those days we were hard up and I used to push a pram round to Mrs Ling's house for mum and sell her second-hand goods.

Margaret Jackson

Yardleys

Yardleys had a belt system which started up directly you got in. A girl sat on each side of the belt and when one of them went for a break they would stop that side but the other side had to keep going. I was on aerosols which was the worst job because every time you put the top on they popped up and you got sprayed. If you could not keep up you took the aerosols off the conveyor belt and you had to do them later when the belt broke down. If you took more than five minutes for a break the supervisor came and got you. I did eight till twelve. Staff were allowed to buy the rejects at a reduced price.

Pat Radley

Southernhay Sculpture

My husband, Tom Wright, was the managing director of C & E Engineering and was respon-sible for the metal sculpture in the underpass at Southernhay roundabout. Tom was a hands-on person and was very accurate working out everything to the last millimetre. While they were constructing the sculpture the workforce wondered how they would get it out through the factory door but my Tom had it all calculated. When they finished it Tom had a crane turn it on its side and it slipped through the door with millimetres to spare.

One Sunday morning they loaded it on a lorry and drove it slowly to Basildon with a police escort stopping the traffic. The site had been prepared the week before and a giant crane gently lifted it into the air, over the rail, dropping it exactly in place just as Tom had planned. When he was serving his apprenticeship Tom worked on the Sir Basil Spence sculpture on Coventry Cathedral.

Rose Wright

Carreras' Catcher Girls

Originally Carreras was started by the Eastend family called Baron, who apart from running Carreras ran the Bernard Baron Settlements for underprivileged families.

Carreras imported tobacco from the West Indies, Rhodesia and Virginia and would blend them together. They had to pay duty on the tobacco but paid more when it did not come

from one of the non-empire countries. The tobacco came in leaf form, in round hogsheads and went into bond. To get it out we had to pay the tax which was as much as £600,000 a day. They did not recoup the money until they had made the cigarettes and sold them. We exported our products all over the world, our biggest market being the Middle East. We made a number of well known brands including, Craven A and Dunhill. We merged with Rothmans and added Rothmans and Consulate to our brands. We were the biggest exporters in the country. Then Carreras found it cheaper to manufacture the cigarettes locally.

Carreras workforce consisted mainly of women who worked on the assembly line but men worked on the export line, because of the heavier weights. The girls were called catcher girls because they were there as the cigarettes came out of the machine. Eventually everything was so mechanised that tobacco went in one end of a machine and cigarettes came out at the other, untouched by human hand.

Bob Ayres

Holloway Lill

Soon after we came down here in 1957 I started work in the Bryn School as a cleaner and then I heard of a job at Carreras and went to work for them from ten till two. It was a good firm to work for and I enjoyed it. Part-timers used to do the packing and relieve on the machines when the full timers went for a tea break.

As a company they were very advanced and you could have a smear test or see the chiropodist and if anybody was leaving or ill they really made a fuss of them. I remember them collecting for a girl who was leaving to have a baby and they bought her everything, a bath, carry cot, everything. Carreras paid well and I earned £10 a week.

Sometimes, a security woman, we nicknamed Holloway Lill, used to take us into a room and search us. The first thing she would do was to make you sit down as people hide things in funny places.

Pat Radley

Opposite: Yardley's
Factory.

Right: Bob Ayres today.

The Big Black Cat

During the sixties I was working for the Basildon Development Corporation when I heard that Carreras were coming to Basildon. I applied and got a post as an export clerk. At first I worked in Mornington Crescent, London and travelled up each day by coach from the town centre but we had to pay, which we thought was unfair because if we had worked in Basildon we would not have to pay fares. We put it to the management and to our surprise they agreed to us travelling free. Then we asked them to pay for travelling time and they agreed to that too. Carreras was a good firm to work for.

Then I transferred to the export department in Basildon. Outside the factory in London were two big bronze black cats and when the factory closed, one cat was shipped to Jamaica and the other one came down to Basildon. When Carreras closed in Basildon I don't know where it went.

In the old days they sacked women if they got married and so, in my opinion, that is why they had so many people devoted to the firm.

The women wore white or blue overalls and the men wore boiler suits.

The staff were allowed to buy cigarettes which were in a differently designed pack and if security caught anyone with a non-staff cigarette they were in trouble. I was promoted and moved up to the sales office at No. 8 Baker Street in London but at about this time they were planning to move their Basildon factory to Aylesbury. It was not the right time for the family to move and so I obtained a position as the house manager with Dunhills, which was part of the group.

Bob Ayres

Training Scheme

I decided to leave the grammar school at fifteen as I wanted to be a secretary or work on a comptometer. I had no idea what a comptometer was but despite this my aunt walked me round the factory estate and called in at all the firms for jobs.

At Carreras I filled in a form and to my surprise they offered me a place on their training scheme. I worked a prototype adding machine.

There were six of us on the scheme which had been running for a year. They sent us to Thurrock Technical School for business studies which included studying organisation and methods. One of the things the school did was to take us on a liner round Tilbury Docks. The course was designed to make us management material and was to give us a good grounding in how the company worked.

Our jobs were going to be to improve the systems by organisation and methods. In those days computers were as big as my dining room and were kept in an air-locked room. Carreras offices were very mechanised.

Sandra Bonnett (*née* Keyes)

Doctor Long

In the early days we only consulted a doctor once and that was when mum got stung by a hornet. I remember going to the surgery and being told I was lucky as the doctor only attended on Tuesday and Thursday and being Tuesday he was there.

There was no National Health in those days and you had to pay. My sister was on the panel and registered with Dr Henderson. When he retired the practice was taken over by Dr Long, who set up his surgery in Hiawatha House on the corner of The High Road and Nicholas Lane.

There was no appointment system and patients would arrive and sit in the surgery, moving up each time until it was their turn. He must have had a scale of charges, as dad had a five-minute consultation and was charged two shillings and six pence whereas I was with him for longer and also had a bottle of medicine and that only cost one and six.

When asking for a home visit, we would advise the doctor on the state of the road and where to park and remind him to bring his wellington boots. When my father was very ill he would call in unannounced while he was walking his dog. If he thought dad needed a prescription he would ask me to call in for it. When an elderly patient once thanked him for calling one evening, he replied 'It is my privilege to do so.'

Elsie Hill (*née* Neville)

Shepherd

My brother worked as a shepherd on Wayletts Farm Basildon for about thirty-five years. People tend to think that sheep take care of themselves but they don't and in summer they have to be looked at every day. If they get dirty round the back end, flies land on it they get maggots in no time at all and so every morning you have to cut that bit of fur away. Twice a year sheep are dipped and you have to push them right under to get rid of the maggots and things. Now and again you have to tip them upside down and cut their nails. If they are left, they cannot walk. The tupps (rams) are worse than the females as they grow twice as fast. In May the sheep are sheared and a man can shear two sheep in ten minutes. The wool is thrown up into a big sack, hung from the ceiling and when full, sewn up. The bundles weigh about three or four hundredweight.

Fred Broom

Working on the Railway

I worked for a firm called Jackerman on the railway lines, when they were converting them from steam to electricity. I helped to raise the bridges in Basildon. They closed the lines on a Friday night and we would work over the weekend until the work was finished.

David Pratt

Decorations on Prams

During the thirties my dad, who was very artistic, used to paint the decorations on prams with a brush that was so fine that it only had a few long hairs. Unfortunately directly war broke out he lost his job. He was very religious and never

Ilfords during the 1960s.

swore. They sent him hop picking and when he came back we found that he was swearing but he would not believe it. So every time he swore I told him and then instead of swearing he would say 'O Beethoven'. At church he played the organ and painted the posters for the church.

Maud Sargeant

Secretary

In 1940 I was fourteen and decided it was about time I went to work. I had a few lessons in shorthand and read the first Pitman's book. Mum then took me up to Columbia Pictures for a job where I was interviewed by Miss Bullock. She gave me a test but I could not do it, I had not had enough practice. It was not till later that I realised how kind she was as she gave me a job. In those early days, when I took down dictation I would write a lot of it in longhand and sometimes sit in the toilet crying. There were no lessons in those days and so I bought some books and learnt shorthand.

The firm moved up to Derbyshire and I went with them obtaining lodgings in a house where the woman did not trust me. I stayed for a while then there was a lull in the bombing and I came back to Basildon and worked in London. I used to travel up by train each day which would take the same time as it does today, an hour, except for the slight rise on the way back at East Horndon where the train had to get up steam. We used to get out of the train and go in the pub where I would meet my father. When the

Factory site during the 1960s.

train got up enough steam it must have blown its whistle as we all climbed back on board.

The late Yvonne Smith (*née* Brasier)

Waitress

When I left school my mother wanted me to do needlework and so I got a job at Bagents in Laindon High Road. It was only a small workshop and they started me off by sewing on buttons and then I gradually progressed to making ladies clothes. I was there for a while and then I obtained a job in a shirt factory in Upminster and used to travel there each day by bus where I earned fourteen shillings a week for working from 8 a.m. till 5 p.m. five days a week. After that I worked for Henbest a haberdashery in the High Road, then I worked as a waitress in Upminster Rooms Store and earned one pound and ten shillings plus tips.

Thelma Broom

Gravy

I used to go up by train each day to Doctor Barnardos in Stepney East where I worked as a shorthand typist writing what we called 'gravy letters' thanking people for their donations. I learnt shorthand at evening classes while I was working at the florists shop.

Maud Sargeant

Working for the Crown

I left school when I was fourteen after having fallen out with one of the teachers. I did not know what I wanted to do and tried a number of jobs before following in my ancestors footsteps. My great-granddad, granddad, dad and uncle worked as builders and in particular, carpenters. First I worked in a glass factory, working on prisms and then I thought I would try my hand at working for a central heating firm who took me on because I could get under the floorboards without taking them all up. Then my father suggested that I went to work for my uncle Reg and my cousin, building. We worked on installing the woodwork in houses, roofing trusses, first and second fixings. I decided to go to evening classes three nights a week at East Ham Technical College to take my City & Guilds in carpentry. In order to take my final examinations, I was supposed to go on day release but the firm would not let me go so, I never took them.

Chriss and I married and moved to Wickford and I started working for Greenhams, who carried out painting contracts for Basildon Development Corporation. I made good any woodwork prior to painting and helped to build two Baptist churches, one in Perry Street, Billericay and the other in Wickford. This was at the time when Basildon Development Corporation was still building the town.

After a time I decided to work for myself but it did not work out and so I started working in a carpentry shop.

Most of our current work is for the Corporation of London which includes Buckingham Palace, Clarence House, American Embassy, Royal Courts of Justice and the National. Everybody has to have security clearance. The most awkward job I have done is a five-metre window.

Roy Hands

Teaching Life Skills

When I left school I worked in a pyjama factory in Upminster and it would take me one-and-half-hours to cycle there and another hour-and-a-half back all for seven-and six pence a week. After I had the children I started work as a carer for the Ashley Centre in Whitmore Way. I taught the handicapped life and domestic skills to enable them to live on their own.

Margaret Read

Member of Parliament

I was born in Islington and my parents came down to Basildon in 1971. I was brought up on the Five Links Estate which had the nickname 'Alcatraz' where I had a very happy childhood. I went to St Nicholas School which later amalgamated with Laindon School. I did a degree at Bristol University and read history. I subsequently went to Kings in London to study war history.

My ambition, right from a small boy was to get into Parliament and in 1991, aged twenty-six years, I was elected as a local councillor for Basildon. I enjoyed the job of serving the people and was selected as a Tory candidate for Brent East to run against Ken Livingstone. I obviously did not get in but gave him a run for his money. In 2000 I was lucky to be selected as a candidate for Rayleigh and was elected in 2001.

Mark Francois MP

We had Three Choices

When I left school in 1949, I had three choices of job – Bata's of Tilbury, who made shoes, Glanvilles at Tarpots, who made shirts, or Woolworth in Southend but I was lucky and landed a job in the local wool shop just up the road where I worked for five years before going to Armand Taylor's over the Pitsea line. They made electrical circuits.

Margaret Browning

Borg Warner

I worked for York Shipley in Nottingham, then in 1964 I heard that the firm was being taken over by Borg Warner and was moving to Basildon. Half the firm was in Cricklewood and the other half was on the Industrial Park Basildon, which was a brand new factory. We made engine blocks for the Lee Frances, a car like the Jag, the cooling system for nuclear reactors and refrigeration units for hotels and ships. For months thirty of us travelled down from Nottingham each Monday to work and returned home on Friday. Finally Basildon Development Corporation allocated us a house in St Nicholas Lane and I watched it being built brick by brick. Then Janet, my wife, came down and we moved in. The firm was really good and paid for all the expenses.

Bob Garrard

Borg Warner.

Magistrates Court

In 1991 Basildon Magistrates court was built and I was one of the first seven magistrates to be sworn in at the new court house. My journey began with a Women's Institute meeting where the speaker spoke about work as a magistrate. A week later I had a discussion with another WI member who was a magistrate and she subsequently telephoned me and asked if I would be interested in applying to be a magistrate. I was taken aback and told her that I did not think it was for people like me. She said that it was exactly for people like me, having commonsense and personal integrity. She arranged for us to sit at the back of Grays Court and then over lunch asked if she could put my name forward, which she did. I completed an application form and sent it off. The first stage then was that three magistrates came to talk to me at home, then they sent me some case papers to study which formed part of a formal interview held in front of a panel at the court house. There was a long wait until eventually a letter of appointment arrived from the Lord Chancellor's Office. The whole procedure had taken fifteen months. The first case I sat on was a drink-drive trial.

Carol Porter (*née* Harris)

Local Councillor

I became interested in politics when I was very young and people tried to persuade me to their left wing views but after listening to their arguments I made up my own mind. I did not like what was happening in Basildon and so I became involved. I was elected in 1979 and at various times I lost my seat and got it back. The first year I was elected I was vice-chairman of Works and I was chairman of the Community Committee and finished up as leader of the council. One of my minor but important achievements was to have all the street signs put up at a high level so that drivers could see the signs from both directions.

What has given me most pleasure over the years is helping people, just small things which they had been unable to achieve on their own.

Vic York

Odd Jobs Man

About 1964 I started work erecting fencing on building sites around Laindon but the work dried up and I was given my cards. I got a job in Barton's Bakery in Basildon, but it wasn't baking bread or cakes like I wanted but was operating a machine on the night-shift and filling doughnuts. I left and started work with South Essex Motors in Cherrydown as a petrol pump attendant. The money was good and the work very enjoyable, with good workmates.

Brian Baylis

Standard Telephone Company

When we moved down from Nottingham I started work for the Standard Telephone Co. as a secretary. At that time they were in Woolwich and they supplied a coach to get us there each day. The old premises were by the side of the docks and were terrible. Each day a little man came furtively through the office carrying a bag and a small club. We all wondered what he was doing, then we found out; he was a rat catcher! One thing I do remember was each day we had hot toast oozing with dripping.

During the sixties STC moved into their new factory in Basildon and we thought we were in heaven after the dilapidated building in Woolwich. We worked hard and sometimes, when the firm was tendering for a new contract, we would work all night to get it.

After a time I realized I could earn more money temping in London and in those days if you did not like a job, you walked out and got another one the same day.

I used to travel from Laindon Railway Station as there wasn't one in Basildon. The trains were always late with excuses like, leaves on the line. In the end I got fed up with travelling and went to work for Steggles, the solicitors in Clock House at the Laindon Centre.

Janet Garrard

Rumours Abounded

When I was fifteen I left Laindon High Road School on 21 December 1961, and have never regretted it. I obtained my national insurance card from Keay House, opposite where W H Smith is now. At first I wanted to be a chef or baker and went for an interview with Cottis's Bakery who said they would be in touch; I am still waiting! Instead I started work for Brown & Tawse Tubes at West Horndon on 3 January 1962 as a telex boy.

While working there the foreman called Sam was always full of rumours. He said that Brooke House in Basildon town centre was starting to lean and everybody was going to have to move out. There was no truth in the story. Another time he said that one of the Chinese Restaurants was caught serving Kit-E-Kat.

Brian Baylis

In Print

When I left school I signed up for a six-year apprenticeship with the printing firm Grant Best of Durham Road, Laindon.

When I qualified I suffered the indignity of the initiation ceremony but unfortunately everyone had to go through it when they passed. I left Grant Best and went to work for Leates at Southend staying there for a while before having a complete change of job and working for a book maker.

Tony Read

Architect

After my National Service I started work in the architects' department at East Ham Council and started studying for my qualifications at Northern Polytechnic four nights a week for seven years.

By this time I had married and we wanted to buy a house and found one in Ravensdale Basildon for £2,700. Unfortunately the owners put the price up but my mother came to our rescue and gave us the extra money.

I started working for Basildon Council but when I qualified they did not have a post for somebody with my qualifications and so I went back to Newham and waited for a suitable post in Basildon. Finally one came up. At that time the staff were split between a wooden building in Fodderwick which was designed by our architects, Key House & Billericay.

Over the years I worked on the swimming pools at Wickford, Pitsea and Billericay. Billericay had some innovative features, such as reusing the heat and recirculating it. Some of the housing projects I worked on were Park Lodge and Craylands.

Craylands Estate was designed on a Swedish idea which cut down on roads, restricting cars, leaving the roads mainly for pedestrians. We were encouraged by the government of the day by larger subsidies. The idea was good and worked for a time until society changed.

I worked on the Wickford Community Centre and the Clinic under Ken Cotton the chief architect. The soil in Basildon was clay and so you either had to put in piles or have a raft.

John Snoding

All I Wanted was to Leave

They wanted me to stay on at school but all I wanted was to leave. My aunt saw an advert in the paper for a commercial apprentice at the Ford Motor Co., Dagenham and I applied. Only thirty out of the 130 who applied obtained jobs. When I started at Fords the only qualifications I had were O and A-levels while some of the other boys had been to grammar schools and colleges. I went to evening classes and studied for ten years and qualified as an accountant. I worked at Fords for six years and before I left I was working on the project at the Dunton Research Centre. I left because I failed some day release examinations and the rule was that

if you failed they would not let you go back to day school and you had to attend evening classes, which I was already doing. I refused and said that I would look for another job. Then somebody at Ford got a post as chief accountant with a private catering company and he offered me a job as his assistant and my salary jumped by a third.

Ken Porter

Fords

I started work in Whitechapel Library in Stepney after a grammar school education and after completing my National Service I went into a menswear shop. By this time I was married and one day on our way to Burnham we saw the houses here in Basildon. We investigated and found out that you had to work here to get one. I obtained work on the assembly line at Ford Dagenham hoping to get a transfer to Basildon. It was hard shift work, a week on nights and then a week on days. It was ironic that we turned out more tractors at night than we did during the day and that was because it was colder. Sometimes, during the night they would open the windows in the roof to make it even colder but we earned good money.

Bob Ayres

The Assembly Line

After I did my National Service I did several jobs and then I went to Ford's tractor plant where I worked on the hydraulic line which was only a little shop. It was hard work and as a new boy you got the difficult work. They would set the line at a certain speed and if you missed any bits they went down a hole. Sometimes they would set the line faster to increase productivity. They did not always take notice of you when you reported a fault and one day we had an inspection by three men in suits who stood by this machine that I had reported was faulty and they got smothered in hydraulic oil.

FORD MOTOR COMPANY LTD.
BASILDON TRACTOR PLANT
Project No: Y/
Consultant : Artek (UK) LTD.
Contractor : G. P. Trentham
View : As Indicated
Date : Photo No

Fords from the air. (Copyright Ford)

Unfortunately I became ill and the doctor told me I should not be on shift work and so Fords put me into the parts department. We used to get orders for parts from all over the world and despatch them. I left to repair washing machines and electrical goods.

Horace Remmington

It was Good Money

I worked for Fords in the seventies and was there for twenty-four years. It was hard work on the main production line making forward axles.

When the line started up at seven in the morning you had to be there on time to clock on. If anybody was late they were taken into the office and warned. A couple of warnings and you were out. If when they started up the line there were not enough men to man it they took them from elsewhere in the factory.

All the time you had to keep to the speed of the line. I did the day shift which was the best one because all the blokes got on and worked well together. It was hard but for those times the wages were good and regular. When I started I earned £35 per week and if I wanted it, there was always plenty of overtime but I never did because of my interest in the Berry Boys' Club.

They had a security man on the gate who searched anybody he thought was stealing. If he found anything, he took them into the office where they were searched, then sacked.

Ford had a good social club where they played bowls, darts and pool and served food. Each

FORD MOTOR COMPANY LTD.
BASILDON TRACTOR PLANT
Project No. Y/8
Consultant : Artek (UK) LTD.
Contractor : G. P. Trentham
View : As Indicated
Date : 6.6.68. Photo No

Part of the works inside Ford during construction. (Copyright Ford)

week they held dances and had entertainers. I took early retirement.

Tony Read

Engineer

I did an apprenticeship with a metal company called Delta Metal Co. which was the biggest in the world. The metal was extruded, which means for example, take a stair handrail, you place a billet of hot brass behind a die and push it through. We did things as small as spectacle hinges.

I went to Fords as a draughtsman and when, on the first day, I put a piece of backing paper in my board my boss shouted out 'Vic I don't want a draughtsman I want an engineer and you are a trained engineer!' and so straight away I became an equipment engineer. At that time they were in the process of building Halewood & Swansea. It was before computers and I had to work out how many furnaces we needed to do a certain task.

I installed production machines but because the operators were on piecework they devised ways to get round the safety gadgets to speed things up. They took chances with their safety.

Vic York

Marconi's

I registered with the Laura Edwards agency for work and they sent me to Marconi's as a filing clerk. I worked there temporarily for a time and

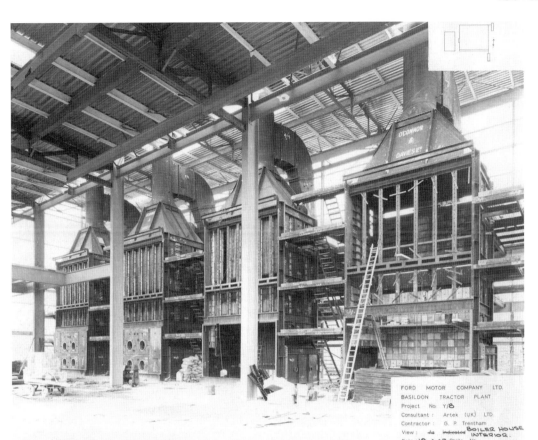

Ford boilers being constructed 1963. (Copyright Ford)

then they offered me a full-time job which lasted thirteen years. We had to clock in each day and if you were a moment late they stopped you a quarter of an hour.

Eventually I became a Progress Chaser and it was my job to ensure parts were delivered on time. Marconi's did a lot of work for the Ministry of Defence making printed circuits for aero space and I would have loved to have seen the end product but I never did.

Pat Radley

Ilford

Ilford, the film and camera producer transferred their manufacturing concern to Basildon from Brentwood in the late fifties and sited the factory on the corner of Christopher Martins Road and Gardiners Lane. I was engaged in many facets of the move. The factory in Brentwood was near the station and as we were about to move, the management were reluctant to spend money on maintenance. The girls, who were unaware of the impending move, continually complained about the lack of heating. The equipment was worn out. The management would only authorise the renewal of bits of piping to try and keep the girls happy.

I did not move to Basildon at that time, instead I had a yearning to visit and work abroad. I tried for Rhodesia but could not find work and then I was offered a post in South Africa

Janet Millwood today.

We stayed there for three years before returning home.

There were no engineering design offices in the Ilford offices at Basildon and so I sought employment elsewhere. The Vange unemployment office directed me to Albert Mann Ltd where I obtained a post in their design office.

Roy Wallis

Dentist and Doctor

I went to the University College Hospital Dentistry School in Great Portland Street for six years to train as a dentist. The school was a decrepit old place with the walls covered in white tiles. I met my husband while I was studying as he was training to be a doctor at UCH Medical School nearby.

We got married and just as he finished his seven years doctors' course he got called up for National Service but signed on for an extra year, which gave him a nice uniform and a little extra money. He served as an Army Medical Officer and was posted just outside York.

After the three years he found it difficult to obtain a post in general practice and then in 1963 we saw a position with Dr Long at Hiawatha House, Laindon. When we came for the interview Laindon looked just like the wild-west, with shacks and unmade sandy roads. Laindon Centre had not been built and the shops along the High Road were all old. All that was missing was the horses tied up. He was offered and accepted the post on a year's probation and we moved into Vowler Road. As the town grew so did the practice, and finally moved into premises at Danacre.

I started work as a dentist at the Laindon Clinic which was below the railway bridge and then, in the later years at Great Oaks. After a school inspection we would send a note home to the parents to say their children's teeth needed attention under the National Health, which was free, but sometimes they did not bring them along for the treatment.

Janet Millwood

Taxi Driver

When they were building the town I was an apprentice and so to earn some extra money I used to drive a taxi for Parkinson and would wait outside Laindon Station for the trains to come in.

David Pratt

Mobile Canteen

When they were building the factories my dad got the contract for supplying all the builders with sandwiches and tea. We used to prepare them in Enefer's Cafe and then drive out in a mobile van to all the sites and the builders used to queue up.

Gayle Pratt

six

Basildon Development Corporation

BASILDON
TENANTS HANDBOOK

Basildon Development Corporation's Legal Department

During the sixties I started working for the Basildon Development Corporation legal department. At first the offices were in the Old Rectory which was near Howard Park in Pitsea, where St Gabriel's church is now. It was a lovely place to work and was set in beautiful grounds. I started work as a shorthand typist and finished up working for Miss Capon, the corporation's solicitor. The general manager in those days was Mr Boniface and Beryl Pygott was his secretary. We did compulsory purchase, road closures and when I worked for Miss Capon I did the legal work on the town centre shops and new licences when they changed shops. It was a happy department and Miss Capon was very loyal to her staff and devoted to her job. She would ring me up on a Saturday and ask me to go in to go through some legal problem. Mr Spinks used to work for the department as did Dave Booty who later went to Basildon District Council.

I and my colleague Margot got a system going and tried to do more work each day. When we started selling the houses to the tenants in the seventies we used to work like mad to see how many sales we could do in a day. There was a backlog of house sales and I worked it out that if we did so many a day we would get rid of them as the general manager wanted them out of the way. Some of the staff were very relaxed and did not work as hard as us. We overcame a number of legal problems in connection with title where people had taken over plots and could not prove that they owned them .Things did not always go smoothly and once we obtained a great machine. In theory, you put in a blank conveyance form and it was supposed to run it off. The idea was to save time. Janet, my daughter went on a two week course to run it but the machine was a complete disaster. In the end the manufacturers came to the conclusion that the electric power was not right. Another time we sold a whole row of houses with their dustbin sheds in the next gardens.

We had several moves to different offices over the years. We moved to Freedom House in the town centre and then finished up in Gifford House.

I received a medal from the Queen during her jubilee year for working for the corporation. I did not agree with it as I think medals should go to people who do things for nothing, not to people who get paid for a job. My husband George framed it for me.

Maud Sargeant

Sexual Discrimination

My first job was with British Petroleum and the girls that I worked with still meet up now, forty years later. In 1958, soon after Bob and I got married, we came down to Basildon to find work and to obtain housing. Bob could not find suitable employment but I saw a job advertised in the housing department of the Basildon Development Corporation. I applied and got an interview. At BP we used to dress very smartly and I wanted to make a good impression and so I arrived at Pitsea station dressed in a very tight navy blue suit, with a pink straw boater. The corporation arranged for Ted Turner, the chauffeur, to meet me, in a Landrover. I had to hoist my skirt up to climb aboard and got the giggles, which lasted all through the interview. Despite this I got the job and started work for the housing department in the White Cafe near the Barge. Ron Hackett was the manager and other staff were Jack Kent, Ted Pengelly, John Radley and Norman Bennett.

I was the only woman and had to answer the telephone on a wind-up switchboard and make the tea. My office was in an undecorated kitchen crawling with ants. Part of our offices were across the road and I had to ring them up and say 'Tea's ready' but because they had to cross the busy road the tea was cold when they got it.

On Fridays, one of our jobs was giving out the keys to the new tenants. Some would cry

Above: Maud with her medal and certificate.

Right: Tenant's handbook. (Copyright Basildon Development Corporation)

with joy and would give us cakes. Outside the office the baker, milkman and coalman would wait to catch the tenants as they came out. It was a lovely place to work.

When they came to allocate accommodation to us I could not believe it, they told me that because I was a woman they could only allocate us a flat. Had I been a man they would have given us a house.

Joy Ayres

Life was Safer

It was very safe in Basildon and in those early days there was hardly any crime. I don't know if it was because we were younger. The housing department at the corporation had a good working relationship with the police, particularly Sgt Tyson who was the coordinator at Basildon Police Station.

John Radley

Cherrydown

The housing office moved from the White Cafe to Cherrydown and I left to have my children but I kept in touch by calling in to see if anybody wanted shopping. In those days they did not have to keep our jobs open during pregnancy. When my sons went to school I went back to work again in the lettings department with Miss Palmer and Miss Lloyd. Mr Dant was the housing manager by then, Mr Crewdson was his deputy and there was Bob Bobin, who was quite an artist.

Joy Ayres

Florist

In the early days at Basildon Development Corporation one of the girls was going to get married and she asked me to do her flowers for her wedding. I wrote to a firm in Cornwall

The Lynge Siporex, 1970s.

They had a lot of problems with the Blue House Estate. The properties were designed in Sweden and were built with a type of concrete blown full of air. Soon after they were built they started to crack up. I can remember going round to one property with a surveyor and seeing a house, all crooked and leaning against the other just like the house that Jack built.

Janet Garrard

and did a course on weddings. When the course came I found I knew most of what they had provided and so I did the wedding. I used to go up to Spitalfields Market at 3.30 a.m. and then on to work at the Corporation. My husband, George, used to do the deliveries. We did all the flowers at Standard Telephones, Yardleys and many other big factories.

Maud Sargeant

Blue House Estate

In 1970 I started work for the maintenance department of Basildon Development Corporation in their Lee Chapel North office.

District Housing Manager

I started work at the Co-op in London collecting rents from flats above the shops. One flat became vacant and I applied for it but it was allocated to someone else. I got so angry that I decided to look for another job. My brother-in-law Tom got a job with the corporation as a painter and decorator and was allocated a house. This encouraged Pat and me to come down to Basildon on Tom's motorbike to look for a job but I could not find one. Then somebody showed me an advert for a rent-collecting job with the corporation. The only problem was that the corporation used the Gilbert system, which was a way of recording rents on the door step. I knew nothing about it. I got an interview but it was a really difficult journey to Basildon.

Left: The start of the Manor Road Development as part of the New Church View Estate in the 1990s, built by Basildon Community Housing Association, now Swan Housing Association.

Opposite below: Basildon Development Corporation Football Team. From left to right, back row: Fred Fowler, Ray Ayre, John Radley, Bert Draper, Stan Merrells, Eddie Petitt, Joe Vincent, -?-, Redman.

Above: Housing Managers relaxing at the GPO Club in the early 1980s after a meeting. From left to right: John Radley, Mike Moss, Reg Winter, Jim Reeve, Jim Coventry, John Payne, Alex Coulson, Norman Bennett.

Some of the staff from Laindon Housing Office, 1980s.
From left to right: Caroline Wilk, Kelly, Maureen Smith,
Julie Woods.

I caught a train, changed at Romford for Pitsea, then a bus to Gifford House. Mr West and Mr Aldous, the housing manager, interviewed me and offered me the job.

I started work in the White Cafe at Pitsea. It is now a building for the blind. I found the Gilbert system difficult but I had a great deal of help from colleagues, in particular Norman Bennett, Norman Lee, Geoff Wray, Sid Franklin and Dick Blisson. They were great. Jack Kent was in charge and Harold Wood was the cashier. The first collection I did was Long Ridding. On a Friday we all piled in the Landrover and went up to Gifford House to collect our wages.

The corporation then built a housing office in Cherrydown near the bus station. The maintenance department had a yard in the Hatherley and an office. The management staff were based in the wooden hut behind it. The next office they built was in Laindon and I went up there with Gerry Cupit. I got promoted to district manager and took over the Fryerns Office. Soon after they built an office at Pitsea and I took it over while Jim Reeve took over Fryerns.

Over the years we evicted some tenants who were bad payers but we gave them every chance. We would do everything to prevent it by making sure they had all the benefits they were entitled to. Some still did not pay and so we would take them to court and the registrar would give them another chance. If they still did not pay we had no alternative but to arrange their eviction. On the day of the eviction the bailiff would attend with the carpenter and we would go in. If the people had not gone we would evict them, telling them that they had a fortnight to collect their belongings. It was very sad but we had given them every chance.

John Radley

Sorry I got it Wrong

We had a very efficient maintenance department but mistakes were made. One of our bricklayers went round to a house to unblock the chimney. He carefully covered the living room with dust sheets and then went up on the roof and dropped a ball down the chimney. As the ball went whizzing down he looked round and saw another chimney; he had dropped it down the wrong one! There was soot everywhere!

Jim Turnbull

Bowler Hats

To make us more efficient Basildon Development Corporation changed from weekly rent collection to fortnightly. One day somebody got attacked while rent collecting and to give us protection they issued us with steel bowler hats but nobody wore them. When it rained it was just like the Chinese water torture treatment.

Rent collectors all over the country were being attacked and to protect the staff and save money they started office collections. The only collections that we did after that were from the OAPs.

The corporation built some nice properties, including some that Sir Basil Spence designed.

John Radley

seven

Basildon at Play

Dodging the Gamekeeper

I have been ferreting all my life and back in the forties I used to go round with my father and set snares in the fields. One night we caught forty rabbits. Sometimes we caught so many that we could not carry them all home and so we dug a hole and buried some of them so the old gamekeeper would not find them and we used to go back the next night, pull back the leaves and dig them up.

We would net up all the holes in the earth and then put the ferrets in and the rabbits would shoot out into the net and you had them. I used to sell some to a butcher in Laindon for a pound each. Years ago I sold them for nine pence each and their skins to the old rag and bone man who gave me four pence each for them. I sold fox fur before it became illegal.

Fred Broom

Armed With A Catapult

I spent many happy hours before the war wandering for miles, armed with a catapult or playing 'Robin Hood' in the woods behind our house.

Albert Lee

Down St Michael's Hill

The kids used to go down Church Hill in Pitsea on their sledges almost to Howard's field. From our flat above Norton's we used to watch them skimming down in the moonlight.

Margaret Browning

Past Times

As children we went to free film or slide shows at Gun Hill Mission, the Methodist church in Brackendale Avenue and the Salvation Army at Vange. We went swimming at Vange Wharf and picked bluebells on One Tree Hill. We belonged

to Pitsea Library which was open in Pitsea School two afternoons a week.

If mum did have any spare money we went to the Broadway Cinema – complete with jam sandwiches and Ministry of Food orange juice. In holidays we played all day, making camps, collecting blackberries and acorns. We picked rosehips out of which they made rosehip syrup and we received four pence a pound.

Margaret Jackson

The Rec

The Rec is at the bottom of New Avenue and it originally had swings, sandpit, slide and paddling pool. I believe the land was owned by an Oxford College. There used to be little bungalows at the top end and it is now covered in bracken and blackberries. You can go through the Rec right up to the top of Crown Hill.

During the spring the woods are covered in bluebells and there is an area where a famous species of wild orchid grows and is jealously guarded. The grass is not cut around it during the flowering season.

Maud Sargeant

Dances on the Lawn

During the fifties the lady in No. 12 Brackendale Avenue, Miss Richards, used to hold garden parties while I watched with my nose pressed up against the fence. In the middle of the garden was a large pond surrounded by trees which would glitter with fairy lights. People would dance on the lawn and I loved the way the women's dresses flared out. After a while Miss Richards would take pity on me and ask me in.

Sandra Bonnett (née Keyes)

Hobbies

In the early days after tea we sat round reading, making rugs, embroidering, knitting, mending

Fred Broom at a tractor rally.

or playing games. All this was done by the light of oil lamps.

Elsie Hill (*née* Neville)

Picnics on Laindon Hill

Sometimes, on a Saturday, a whole crowd of us children would take our picnics up to Laindon Hills and play in the sandpits. We would be there until late afternoon when we would all wander home as safe as houses. At other times we got our bikes out and cycled to Maldon and swam in the open air pool out to the two rafts in the centre.

Roy Ives

Fishing for Sticklebacks

When they were building Laindon Link I was playing soldiers in the mounds of earth when one of my friends threw a grenade of earth which hit me straight in the eye and I ran home crying. Another time dad came to get us for dinner when suddenly somebody saw an adder and we froze in fear. Dad grabbed a stick and killed it. I can remember him holding it up on the end of the stick.

There was a pond on Bluehouse Farm where my friends Martin, Barry and I would sneak and fish for sticklebacks, hoping that the farmer would not chase us off with his dogs.

Brian Baylis

Radion cinema, Laindon.

Early Social Activities

We went to Horndon and Bulphan for our social activities where dad joined the British Legion and served on the village hall and flower show committees. I belonged to the Girl Guides. We held dances to raise funds and occasionally we would go to dances in the hall at the back of the Crown Hotel.

Mr George Sibbons, a close neighbour, held whist drives in his games room. There were two sessions and by the second one there would be about thirty people. He charged sixpence a session and the prize money was divided between the winning lady and gentleman.

Elsie Hill (née Neville)

The Flea Pit

In 1964 there was very little entertainment in Basildon but there was the cinema at Laindon, which we called the flea pit and a bowling alley in Southernhay.

As there was a lack of sports I started up a football team at Borg Warner. After twisting the arm of the firm they built us a changing room. We played in the Essex Business Houses League and won the cup a couple of times and came top of the premier division. Once we won the Victoria Cup.

Bob Garrard

Berry Boys' Club

The boxing club was formed by Fred Nunn in 1946. He was a lighterman and lived in Berry Lane. His idea was to take the kids off the street and at first they met over Laindon Hills recreation ground, where he taught them boxing. After a while he managed to obtain the church hall in Salisbury Avenue where I joined in 1949. The

Scouts' band, Manor Mission, during the 1930s.

atmosphere and enthusiasm was electric and Fred was an inspiration to us all. We used to box clubs like Southend and Colchester.

Over the years we have had some really good boxers like Stuart St John who won a heavy-weight title four years ago. Another of our boys got to the finals of the cruiserweight two years out of three. We have had so many successes including ABA champions. When I joined there were only twenty members, and today we have a lot more than that.

The boys don't start boxing until they are eleven years old. We have three classes. The beginners are about ten years old and we start them off with the basics. Before they start boxing they have a medical to make sure they are fit to box. Next we have the second class, they go up to sixteen, and then there is the senior class. A lot of care is taken over the youngsters. Although the sport is criticised it has a very good record. The boys are matched for weight, age and ability. In the early days we did not have headguards as they do today. They start with three one-and-a-half minute rounds and then, as they get older, they have two three-minute rounds. After sixteen they can have up to four three-minute rounds. When I first started to box we had three-minute rounds. Some of our boys have turned professional, John and David Hamm and Mark Quirey who is back as a trainer. We have five trainers who are all vetted etc as they have to be these days.

Today there is not only the boxing club but we also have football teams who do well and play in the local leagues. We are self-financing with raffles etc and we do get some money from the Sports Council. When I joined the club they charged very little and today we charge the seniors £2.00 a night and the youngsters £1.

I have been on the Essex County Committee for the last twenty five-years and am chairman

Borg Warner football team in the 1960s.

of Essex ABA. I am one of the top amateur boxing officials in the country and judge in all the championships. I used to referee but my main job now is the official in charge; that means that I am responsible for weighing in all the boxers and for making sure they are matched correctly.

Tony Read

Motorbike Club

I used to go to a motorbike club in 1956 which was held in Laindon School. It was part of the youth club.

David Pratt

Queen's Coronation

I remember the Queen's Coronation in 1952 when they held a great party in Howard's Park. There was a real carnival atmosphere and everybody got dressed up in their best clothes and they held competitions.

Margaret Browning

Airfix

On a Saturday I would get my two shillings pocket money and I could not wait to get another Airfix construction kit to add to my model railway. In those days, they cost about one shilling and a tube of polystyrene glue cost sixpence. Sometimes I overspent and had to walk home.

Brian Baylis

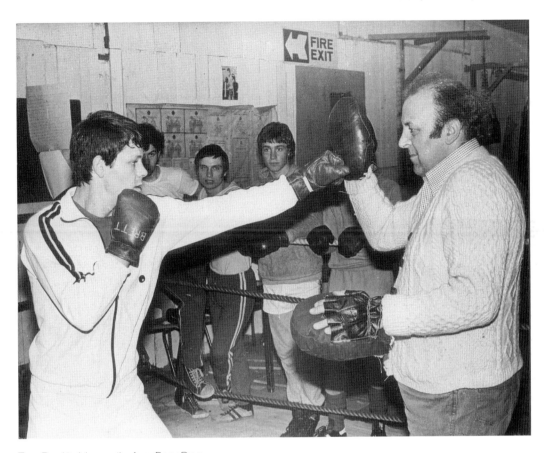

Tony Read training youths from Berry Boys.

St Nicholas Club

When I was young I went to St Nicholas Church Club where we played table tennis, pool, went out on outings and had dances. Later, after I met my husband, I helped out in the Berry Boys Club and we opened it for girls as there was not much for them to do. At that time the club met in the old fire station at Laindon where there was a lot of room. We held fetes at the Laindon Hotel to raise money for the club. I was involved with the catering or was the one they threw the wet sponges at. The boys did a sponsored run from Chelmsford Prison, pushing a bed. During a boxing match I sometimes helped to get the water and have held the bucket while the boys spat in it.

Maureen Read

The Corporation's Sports Teams

When I went to collect my wages at Gifford house I met staff from other departments and while we waited we talked and decided to start a football and cricket team. We were very poor footballers until Eddie Stevens came out of the Royal Air Force and joined us. Another good player was Fred Pennycook. We played in the Southend and District League but then the Basildon League was formed and we joined them and were quite successful. I played mainly in defence and centre half. We had a good captain in Joey Mulcahy.

John Radley

Left: Winning Berry Boys during the late 1970s.

Opposite: Picture of lads at motor bike club/, 956. From left to right, back row: Brian Marshall, Dave Pratt, Malcolm -?-, -?-, Clive -?-, Berney Whitmill. Extreme right: Colin Smith. Front row: Peter O'Rourke, Kenny Vinner, -?-, Smith, Dicky Gordon, -?-.

Hunting

Before the war my father would go out and hunt game with an ancient twelve-bore shotgun and we would dine royally on rabbits, ducks, pheasant and anything that came in range. Unfortunately one day the gun blew up in his face.

Albert Lee

Post Office Club

Bert Hull came from Lancashire, where his life revolved round social clubs. He became the postmaster of Basildon and set up the Post Office Club in 1968 when he got Eddie Robinson to run it as club secretary.

When the club started it was for postmen only but a lot of them did not join so the committee decided to open it up to Basildon Development Corporation, the Tax Office and HMSO. The committee at that time consisted of Alex Hewitt and Eddie Robinson and a number of others. A few sceptics said that the club would not last a fortnight but it's still going today.

At first the club was held in the canteen of the post office, then Bert Hull offered the old sorting office in Laindon, which was opposite the Laindon Hotel. The club was somewhere to relax of an evening and weekends by playing darts, snooker, cards, bingo, had acts and held

fancy dress dances plus they sold drinks at rea-sonable prices. At that time I lived in Newberry Side and could nip out and be in the club in a few moments.

The club was there for a number of years but had to move because Basildon Development Corporation wanted the land to build Great Oxcroft on. Bill again came to the rescue and offered us a floor in the town centre. We were there for a number of years and then we moved to Gardiners Way into a club house we designed ourselves.

Jim Turnbull

Allotments

I've had three allotments in Basildon for years and show some of my vegetables in local shows. Last year I put some leeks in the Billericay show and was a runner-up. My wife never has to buy vegetables as I've always kept the family and some of the neighbours, especially the old ones, supplied.

Fred Broom

Laindon and District Horticultural Society

I am the chairman of Laindon & District Horticultural Society which has been going

for over fifty years. Originally we were down at the Laindon Memorial Hall and then when they built the centre at the back of Toomey's we moved in there. When that got burnt down by vandals we had several other venues but when the community centre was built we moved in there. We meet every month on the third Tuesday at 8 p.m. and have two shows every year. In January I do a garden quiz and then throughout the year we have speakers and a gardeners' question time.

Maud Sargeant

Snooker Club

When I joined the GPO Club in 1971 I found that they were running a singles' snooker competition and Cecil Dant the housing manager won it that year. Snooker was getting a lot of exposure on television and public interest grew and as it did our membership increased and so I put it to a few of the players, like John Radley and Ron Reeve that we formed a club. I acted as secretary and we finished up with fifty-odd members and a waiting list. A number of other organisations like the police, and Basildon Development Corporation and later the fire brigade put in teams and we formed Basildon Services Snooker League. Later Rayleigh Police joined and we finished up with about seven or eight clubs playing in the league and it is still running today. One year my dad Arthur, who was a good player, and I won the doubles.

Jim Turnbull

Above: Post Office Club Tramps Ball, 1968.

Right: Fred Broom's onions.

Opposite: Laindon Carnival, 1930s.

Father Arthur and son
Jim, winning the doubles
competition during the 1970s.

The Basildon Cricket Club

I came down to Basildon in 1958 and started playing football for the Basildon Development Corporation with people my wife Joy worked with, like John Radley, Ted Dossiter and Ron Williams. Harold Wood, somebody else who worked with my wife, belonged to Basildon Cricket Club. I used to study the cricket results in the *Basildon Recorder*. The paper used to be sent to us in London for the job adverts. As a result when I came down here I knew most of the cricketers' names.

When we got the flat in Basildon I sent Peter Lucas, who was sports editor for the *Basildon Recorder*, my cricket CV. He was the fixtures secretary of Laindon's Cricket Club and he recommended me to Basildon Cricket Club. I started playing for them in 1959. In those days there were no leagues and we fixed up friendly matches.

Each year they held a knock out competition which we won seven times. We got on very well with a side called Basildon Cranes and we helped one another out with players. If they were players short we would lend players to one another. It got to the stage where the club was not going anywhere and we were stagnating so we had talks with Basildon Cranes and finally amalgamated and became The Basildon Cricket Club.

We entered into The Lillywhite Frowd League, won our division the first year and, as a result, got promoted. Now we are playing in the Shepherd Senior Essex League. The club has over 100 members. We run four teams on Saturday and one on Sunday.

We bring on the youngsters and have under-eleven, under-fourteen, under-fifteen and under-sixteen teams. We have fifteen qualified coaches in the club. On the Tuesday night when England won the Ashes we had seventy youngsters turn up. At a recent award ceremony, out of the twenty-six awards, twenty were previous youth members.

Each year, to introduce the kids to cricket we hold, with the help of the council and county council, a one-day cricket tournament in which a lot of the local schools take part and last year we had seventeen schools take part.

Winners of the Post Office snooker team. From left to right: Jim Turnbull, Terry Spooner, Frank McManus, Charley, Arthur Turnbull.

This year we started a women's team and our granddaughter Charlotte plays for them.

One of our youngsters, Rubin Herbert, who came from the Cape, finished up playing for Essex.

Bob Ayres

Raising Money for the Cricket Pavilion

The council owns Mopsies Park and the cricket club rent the ground off them. The pavilion belongs to Basildon Cricket Club and was financed by fund-raising. We wrote off to football clubs like Arsenal, Spurs, Chelsea and Essex County Cricket Club and they all sent us things to raffle. Graham Gooch sent us a pair of cricket gloves. Basildon Council gave us an interest free loan out of the distribution fund and slowly we found the £27,000 it cost to build the pavilion.

We now need to build a bigger one because of our increasing membership and the change in legislation. When we started in 1958 our annual subscriptions were £1.50, they are now £60 for adults and £20 for juniors. In the old days we could hire a coach for £35 to go down to Margate to play and would charge each member 75p each, now a coach costs £300.

Bob Ayres

Behind the Scenes

I spent a lot of time involved with my husband's cricket. I did the teas and kept score. I was on the cricket committee and on the Basildon Sports Council.

The whole family is involved. One of my daughters-in-law is the bar manager and the girls do the teas. We have had a good, busy social life in Basildon and I have found that people who say there is nothing to do did nothing before they came here.

Joy Ayres

Laindon Cricket Club

A few of us boys used to get together and play cricket in the street after school and would get a chair from the scullery and put it in the road for a wicket. Sometimes we would walk round

Basildon Knock-out Cup winners, 1968.

The Ladies' Cricket team.

the north side of St Nicholas church and play on Donaldson's school field. One day the head-master from the school spotted us playing and asked 'Who is that knocking the ball all over the place?' I replied 'It was either me or my mate.' He then asked 'Have any of you got white trousers?' What a question to ask, none of us had cricket whites. He then told us Laindon Cricket Club was short of players and asked would we like to play for them? They played at Basildon Country Club, which is now the Irish Club.

Proudly I told my dad and he said that a man he travelled up to work with called Mr Lovell, and who had a wooden leg played for Laindon. I found it difficult to believe but it was true. I went on to get coaching at Ifords from some Essex players. I left Laindon club and joined Ilford Cricket Club.

Ken Porter

Eversley Road Pitch

The football and rugby pitches took many years to bring up to standard. One of the worst was Eversley Road pitch. After a week of heavy rain I trudged up the muddy path to the changing shed. The two teams of Pitsea and Benfleet were standing around waiting for me to inspect the pitch, which I did and declared it fit to play on. After a time the touchlines were barely visible. I sank into the mud and declared that the pitch was unfit to play on but both teams implored me to allow them to play on for another half-hour. When I got home my wife made me take my clothes off outside.

Roy Wallis

A Bucket of Cold Water

All the factories along Cranes Farm Road had sports facilities. The Sports Council had representatives from every sport in the town, ranging from golf, tennis, football, cricket, the whole lot. I was nominated by the Referees'

Football Association to sit on the sports com-mittee. The Sports Council were responsible for the swimming pool, golf club, squash club and the running track. There was controversy over the swimming pool because it was not built to Olympic standards, all it needed was a few more feet.

They set out football pitches in Gloucester Park but there were no changing facilities. The Referees' Association collected money to build them but they did not have any running water, only a bucket.

Roy Wallis

Tobacco Trades Cup

Carreras played in the Tobacco Trades Cup which was a knockout competition and was a great day out. We played at various venues and I played football and cricket.

Bob Ayes

Football Leagues

There were two leagues and in the first, the players enjoyed the game but had not perfected their skills and then there was the Basildon District League. They had five divisions but at one time you could not play on a Sunday. One year Lee Chapel North was in the national cup semi-finals. I used to play football for Hainault and scored a wonderful goal but the referee dis-allowed it because he had blown his whistle for the end of the game. I thought I can do better than him and so I took up refereeing.

One week I would referee and the next I would play. I refereed for thirty-one years but in the end I had very little interest in the game, I did it for the exercise. I think people referee for one of three reasons; some people like to exer-cise their authority over other people and they can do that on the football field, some see it as a way of keeping fit while others love football. In the old days nobody did it for the money. I

used to receive seven shillings and sixpence to cover fares, washing, everything. Once I refereed at Southend and claimed ten shillings and they queried it. I explained that I had a return fare to Laindon Station, and then the bus fare to the ground. I told them that if I had claimed my full expenses it would have cost them twelve shillings and six pence.

Referees have a lot of power and one day I was refereeing a junior match at Wickford when a blonde woman on the sideline started swearing like a trooper. I asked her to curb her language but she would not and so I stopped the game and asked the park keeper to escort her off the ground. She could not believe it.

Roy Wallis

Exercise Clubs

I started going to the exercise clubs about thirty years ago and still go three or four times a week. We used to perform exercises to music and we went all over the place like the Cliffs Pavilion in Southend.

Sadie Turnball

Pitsea Cinema

The only cinemas were in Laindon and Pitsea and one night I went to the Granada in Pitsea with my sister. They seemed to have only one member of staff. He sold us the ticket, then took it at the door and the next moment he was behind us with a torch showing us to our seats. It's now a Bingo Hall.

In 1970 the cinema opened in the town centre and I started work in their restaurant but I did not like the Sunday working and gave it up.

Pat Radley

Above: Sadie Turnbull's exercise club. Sadie is sixth from left.

Opposite: Winners of the Moco Trophy. From left to right, front row: Malcolm Dewar, Eddie Stevens, Peter Smither, Don Gazzard, John Radley, John Risby. Back row: Peter Marshall, Tony Norris, Joe Vincent, Ken Horlock, Jim, Alex Huett, Bob Ayres.

Stamp Collecting

As a school boy I started collecting stamps and was encouraged by my father who took me to Petticoat Lane every Sunday to buy them and my interest continued in the RAF.

When I came out of the forces and started work for Basildon Council. Arthur Hobbs, who was the chief assistant of the Council, Ernie Summer-Hayes, myself and another person started up a stamp club in 1968 but we could not involve people outside and so we opened up our club to others and met at Woodlands School. I used to collect Australian airmails but it got to a stage where I could not afford it and so I started to collect Scouts' stamps from all over the world.

John Snoding

Junior Queen, Lee Chapel South

In about 1964 Lee Chapel South formed a community association. Stan Blackbourne was chairman and was the chief accountant for the Rolling Stones. In May 1967 they decided to have a junior queen and my daughter Gail was elected and crowned by Bill Wyman, one of the Rolling Stones. The national papers printed a photograph of her the next day.

Roy Wallis

A Visit from Prince Philip

I can't remember the exact year, but the schools were closed and we were taken to see Prince Philip near Marconi's. It was the first time I had seen a helicopter and I can remember wishing I could fly in one. Later I achieved my ambition and flew in one like the Prince's.

Brian Baylis

Forgotten Dreams

I used to go and see the Dave Clark Five at the Locarno and it inspired me to try to form a pop group. I went into a shop in East Walk that sold musical instruments and saw a Blue Futurama guitar for £35. I longed for it but on £2.10s a week I could not afford it, not by the time I had given my mother my keep and fares. I kept promising myself, I would eventually save enough money to buy it but never did.

Brian Baylis

Some Clubs in Basildon

Basildon had the feel of a new town when we came here in the sixties and we helped to start a number of clubs such as the poetry society which originated out of a discussion group. We had a music club which was held in an ordinary house in Furrowfelde, people came in to play the piano. The Basildon Towngate was a great institution and was well supported. They had orchestras, plays, ballets and local groups. Downstairs they had four rooms where they held painting and pottery classes and held exhibitions. Upstairs they had a bar.

At Laindon there was the Radion Cinema whose seats were not tiered but when it was refurbished with proper cinema seats the old ones were taken down to the Towngate. The Natural History Society started in the late sixties and still meet today and has monthly talks. They meet at the Laindon Community Centre and have work parties and outings. My husband Anthony was chairman and I am still a member to this day.

Janet Millward

Women's Institute

I went to the WI in Luncies Road where they held cake competitions which I never normally entered nor did my sister. One day she came round and together we cooked a cake. We put it in the competition and to our surprise we won first prize.

Pat Radley

Right: Al Mannigter, Roy Hands and Chris Bearson at the Blues Club.

Opposite: 'The Mikado' starring Joan Sims.

Time Off for Women

I started giving talks to groups and regularly give a flower arranging talk to a group of senior ladies called Time Off For Women who meet at the Bascentre. It used to be held in December and I did arrangements with fresh foliage but they meet in November now and so I do it with artificial material. It is surprising the number of people that I have done wedding flowers for. I was once giving a talk at the WI and the chairman asked me to go on the platform and as I did she said: 'Maud, you did my wedding flowers,' and two people passing my garden said to me, 'Hello Maud, do you remember you did our wedding flowers?' I used also to make and decorate wedding cakes.

Maud Sargeant

Laindon Operatic Society

I understand that it was in 1930 that Laindon Operatic Society started and Mr Holland was one of the founder members. My grandfather Frederick Pitts, my grandmother Beatrice, aunt Gladys Pitts and uncle Derek Pope belonged to the society in those early days. Nan made the teas. Granddad had one or two leading parts but as he got older he started doing the scenery. In the fifties they used to perform at Laindon High Road School and I used to go and see the shows which used to get packed. My cousins Anne Pope and Margaret Pitts joined the company about this time and Joan Sims started her career with the Laindon Players.

Ken Porter

A Real Romance

John: In 1955 I joined Laindon Players at Laindon High Road School, which is where I met my wife.

Ann: I used to go to evening classes for pottery and after we met I joined the Laindon Players and did the stage management. One of the plays we put on was *An Inspector Calls*. We put on three plays a year, Wednesday, Thursday, Friday and Saturday nights. The plays were carefully rehearsed and although we had good attendances

we did not make much money. We also used to run dances and one year somebody made contact with Kenny Ball who attended a dance at the Laindon Community Hall.

John and Ann Rugg

Dave Clark Five

After I started work I used to go to Basildon Locarno practically every Thursday, Saturday and Sunday nights to see the Dave Clark Five. I became a big fan of theirs before they turned professional. After they turned professional, they

Right: John and Barbara Snoding at World Scout Jamboree, Holland, 1995.

Opposite above: Scouts on Kingston Ridge during the 1970s.

Opposite below: 1st Laindon Scouts 1938, outside Laindon Hills Methodist church.

became known as the Tottenham Sound, but I refused to accept this and insisted they were the Basildon Sound.

Brian Baylis

Blues at the Fortune Of War

Before it was knocked down, four of us started a live blues club at the Fortune of War in Laindon and we now have nearly 600 members. Over the years Chris Pearson, John the Hat, Jim, the Harp, Eddie, Mark Gardner and I have organised the bands. When they knocked the Fortune of War down we founded the Council Club at Barleylands. Each Saturday we have different live groups, including some famous ones.

Roy Hands

Kingston Ridge

I joined the Scouts in London during the war and when we moved here somebody asked me to run a troop and said it would not involve more than two hours a week. That turned into

seven days a week! I started as an assistant Cub Scout leader and then moved on to a group scout leader and then eventually to district commissioner. There are not as many scout groups in Basildon now. In those days we had over a 1,000 members. I am president of the Ninth, which is the local group in Kingswood. We have lost quite a lot of the groups over the years and it is my opinion this happened because we originated a lot of the activities which other organisations have copied. At one time we ran a football league which was quite big. An old West Ham manager presented the prizes. We stopped it because some of the parents got too vocal and took the spirit of our ideals away. The kids still like to camp out and camping is always popular. We have our own camp at Kingston Ridge off Staneway.

Some of the earlier groups in Basildon were the Fobbing Group, the Holy Cross Group and Whitmore Way.

John Snoding

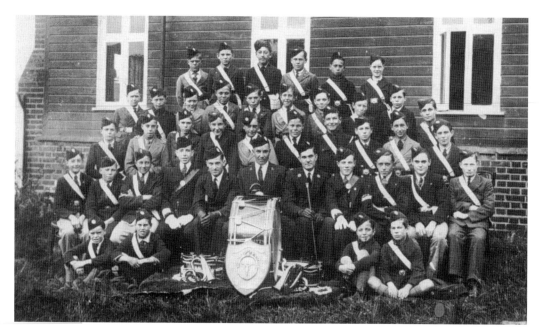

Laindon Boy's Band.

Girl Guides District Commissioner

I had been in the Guides since 1952 and when I got to Basildon in 1963 I had a lady on my doorstep asking me if I would like to join. I took a company at first and we used to meet in the St Nicholas' old wooden church hall, then we moved to what is now James Hornsby's.

I became the district commissioner for Laindon and Langdon Hills. We had Brownies, Guides, Rangers and later Rainbows. Basildon Development Corporation rented us a camping site below the Crown Public House for five pence a year and then somebody allowed horses on it so we lost it.

A Jamboree was held near Walton-on-the-Naze and my daughter came with me. We thought it would be wonderful mixing together but we were allocated a very small part of the camping field. We had one or two incidences where we had to go out to some of the girls in the middle of the night because they had overeaten and were being sick.

The guide movement has changed over the years to incorporate things that modern girls are interested in, like computing, various outdoor pursuits, canoeing, climbing and abseiling. Girls can take the Queen's Guide Award. They have to work hard over a number of years to achieve it.

Janet Millwood

4th Laindon Girl Guides

I belonged to the 4th Laindon Girl Guides and Mrs Freeman was our leader. Once we camped behind the Gun Public House at Pitsea and we were disturbed by the drunks late at night. We went by 2A bus and another time we went by a 53 bus to Jaywick which took three-and-a-half hours. We had a great time cooking our food on an open fire and sleeping in old army tents.

Ann Rugg (*née* Bullimore)

6 FORDHAMS BUILDERS OUTING

Fordham builders' outing in the 1920s.

Guard of Honour

Barbara and I married in 1958 and the Ninth Basildon Brownies formed a guard of honour.

John Snoding

Tub Club

When I was twelve I went to St Nicholas Hall to the Tub Club every Friday night. This was a church club where we played table tennis and just enjoyed ourselves. I went there until I was sixteen. On some nights there were as many as sixty people.

John Rugg

Laindon Cinema

I remember the Radion Cinema in Laindon. There used to be three programmes a week, Monday to Wednesday, then Thursday till Saturday then on Sunday. On Saturday mornings they had the children's matinees. All the kids would roar with excitement. I loved the musicals and remember Roy Rogers. They had a serial each week which ended with the goody in danger so that you would want to go the following week.

Gayle Pratt

Netball

My daughter, Kelly, played netball for England. Like me she went to Pitsea School and then to Chalvedon School where she played netball. She then had trials for Essex. In 1999 she started to play county matches and one day while she was playing, a scout spotted her. She had a number of trials and got into the English team. She went out on tour to the Cook Islands.

Sandra Bonnett (*née* Keyes)

Basildon Badminton

I am chairman of Basildon Badminton Association and league match secretary. In the early days we had loads of leagues and we still run a few now

On the left, Vic York winning gold.

from September to April. We play as far away as Brentwood and Upminster. I play at Woodlands School and was chairman of my old school's association. I also played badminton for Essex County Veterans when I was sixty.

When I was young I used to jump for my school at Barking and got through to the Essex sports. I won a gold, silver and bronze for badminton at the World Masters Games. They have various grades from social players, players who play for the league or county and there are international players. In Melbourne they had 25,000 sportsmen from many countries of the world. The age groups competing were from thirty-five up to ninety-nine. The games range across every sport and a ninety-nine-year-old man ran with the torch to light the flame.

Vic York

eight

Some Basildon Churches

The Holy Mile

There were two main churches in Laindon and Langdon Hills, St Mary's and St Nicholas, but there were many other denominations who built their places of worship in the heart of the communities, where there was a need. These churches and halls became the real centre of the community, providing many cultural and social activities. Other social groups were The British Legion, St Johns Ambulance, The Revellers Concert Party, The Berry Boys Club, the St John's Glee Club and The Laindon Operatic Society. Many of these built their own halls.

The road from Bebbingtons Corner to Laindon Station was known as The Holy Mile and had St Mary's church Hall, The Corner Stone church of Canada, the Roman Catholic church, a Baptist church, Kingdom Hall, a Methodist church, a Pentecostal church, the Ebenezer chapel and across the road the Salvation Army.

Most churches held their services at the same time and the road was thronged with people in their Sunday best. During the Second World War the German prisoners worshiped in the old St Mary's church in Church Hill.

Elsie Hill (*née* Neville)

Jehovah's Witness

I went to St Nicolas church when I was young but it did not make sense to me and then, after I married, a Jehovah witness called round and finally I became a Jehovah witness in 1951 and was baptised in Ipswich. They have meetings in Tylers Avenue Laindon Link and about ninety people attend.

Thelma Broom

Dunton Church

When we first moved on to the plotlands we wanted to go to the church right out in the wilds at Dunton but we found it was falling down and was all netted off. I was so disappointed as I really wanted to go to a quiet country church.

Maud Sargeant

Married in Wellington Boots

I got married in St Michael's church, Pitsea but to get to it you had to walk from the High Road up the steep slope to the church. Sometimes the bride had to go up in her wellington boots and often, when it was very windy, they would lose their head-dresses.

When they had funerals they had to push the coffins up on a bier.

Margaret Browning

Christmas Parties

At Basildon Development Corporation Jo Greenleaf and Dave started holding Christmas parties for the kids at the Baptist church in Clayhall Road. All the corporation kids received a present.

John Radley

Manor Mission

The only churches in Laindon during the 1800s were St Nicholas on the Hill, St Mary's, and the old parish church in Dunton. When the East Enders came down some had been brought up as Baptists, Methodist or at the London City Missions and did not like the orthodox religions or the fact that most of the orthodox churches were some distance away. As in those days everybody walked or rode in a horse and cart they decided to build something nearer, hence The Manor Mission, built in 1907.

It started in a simple manner with Sunday school which grew until the parents wanted an evening service. In the end the attendances got so big that they had to find a piece of land on which to build a bigger mission. Margaret Dell owned a piece of land which she very gener-

St Nicholas church. (Copyright Basildon History Society)

Congregation of Manor Mission, 1920.

Weslevan Methodist church Laindon, 1931.

ously gave to the church and we built the present building on it for £600.

Roy Ives

The Mission's Activities

The Manor Mission in the earlier days had Girl Guides, Brownies, Scouts and Cubs. Then, due to lack of leaders, the mission had only Guides, Brownies and Rainbows.

The mission used to have a round, closed fire to heat the building which would get so hot that the Guides used to roast chestnuts on top. The mission also had a Scout's band which was run by Mr Greatrex.

In the thirties people were really hard up and to help them the mission started a Brotherly Love Fund by donating money.

For the women of the church we started a club which they called the Women's Own and they met one afternoon a week.

Roy Ives

Laindon Spiritualist Church

I became interested in spiritualism and started to attend church. My partner drew my attention to an article in a church magazine which said that Laindon Spiritualist church had a medium.

I wrote to the church and asked if anybody remembered me. By return post I had a reply enclosing a newspaper cutting which advertised people trying to make contact with one another. I wrote to the paper and was surprised by the number of replies I had. I had been to school with one of the replies with whom I had wanted to make contact for years.

We arranged a reunion and what a great night. I especially enjoyed meeting my school mate Tony James who I sat next to in school. Later my favourite teacher, Mr George Poole, rang me. I have nothing but respect for this man.

Brian Baylis

St Basil's Church

My father-in-law Mr O'Leary, built many of the buildings in Basildon, including my house and St Basil's church.

Vic York

nine

Basildon in Uniform

Gassed in the First World War

My dad was gassed with mustard gas in the First World War and so he made sure it was not going to happen to us during the Second World War. The first big raid we had we were straight down our gas proof Anderson shelter in the garden with my dog. A bomb hit an old Victorian school across the road to our house and blew out the windows and doors. My grandmother was lucky because she did not normally go down the shelter but this day, she did. I had just washed my hair and had not had time to rinse it.

When there was a loud bang my dad used to count the seconds until the next one so he could tell how far away it was. They dropped the bombs in sticks but this time they only dropped the one. I cannot remember being frightened but I was worried about our canary who was in the house. When we returned to the house we found he was covered in glass but was all right.

Next morning my great aunt knocked on the door and gave us the keys to a plotland bunga-low on Primrose Hill Estate off Northumberland Avenue. We came down by train piled up with everything including my tortoise, cat and dog. We walked from the station to the bungalow. When we arrived, we opened the cat's cage and it leapt out and shot up the chimney and was there for two days. My dad worked in London on war damage and gradually brought our things down and the rest was put in store which unfor-tunately got bombed.

I was thirteen when we came down but I never went back to school.

The late Yvonne Smith (*née* Brasier)

Killed in the Last Year of the First World War

My father was born in East Ham and at the start of the First World War he and his three broth-ers joined the army and fought in France. In the last year of the war his brothers were killed and he was badly wounded and brought back to England and spent two years recovering in the Middlesex Hospital. The nurses used to take the wounded men over to a local park to play football and that's where he met my mother.

Roy Ives

They Shot Him

During the First World War my father, Joseph Walter Brasier volunteered for the Royal Engineers. There was no need for him to go as he was in a reserved occupation, working on aircraft. He said the war was horrific and related the story of a young soldier who deserted. They caught him and after a court martial sentenced him to death and took him out and shot him. Years later I heard on the radio that this young soldier had been cleared.

My father went through the whole war unscathed except that he got trench fever as a result of being buried for three long days in a trench which had been hit by a shell. He was lucky because a doctor diagnosed it and although he used to get very high temperatures he still lived till he was ninety-three.

The late Yvonne Smith (*née* Brasier)

The Day War Broke Out

In 1939 my mum sent me down to get the accumulator charged for the radio and on the way I met one of my teachers who very excit-edly said 'You had better go home Fred and tell your mother the war's broken out.'

Fred Broom

Teenage Years at War

My teenage years were mostly lived with crump of guns and wail of sirens and nightly treks to cold dark shelters where songs were sung to drown the chaos. Mother, father, sisters and brothers were made doubly precious with the danger that could eclipse our lives for ever but

Reg Hymas' unit resting, 1916.

71 Company Field Day at Laindon during the First World War.

Enifer's Cafe with the other cafe in the background. It was a meeting place for soldiers and their girlfriends.

there were also brighter times when friends gathered round the fireside while someone strummed the old piano and the room would fill with laughter of boys and girls whose hearts were light because of simple pleasures shared in that loved place we called home.

October, February and Christmas were highlights in our teenage journey when we had tremendous parties where, despite the wartime rationing mum would work a miracle and thirty hungry teenage children would sit down to sandwiches, trifles, cakes and lemonade.

The door was always open and neighbours, uncles, aunts and cousins would often share our family pleasures. Countless friends from near and far spent happy weekends playing games, cycling on our bikes to Maldon or rambling up to One Tree Hill.

Friendships forged in far off days have stood the test of time and still we meet and reminisce of joys once shared at Dorisdean and bless the patient loving parents who made our young lives memorable in oh, so many ways.

Betty Morley (*née* Ives)

Gun Emplacement

In the middle of the roundabout of the Fortune of War was a gun emplacement made of steel with barbed wire round it, which we used to climb into. When it rained it would fill up with water and we would splash about in it in our wellington boots. If the Germans invaded they were expected to drive straight up the Southend Road.

Gayle Pratt

Morrison Shelter

The war started when I was nine. Mum found a place in Leytonstone and I helped to move them there on a pram We had an air-raid shelter in the garden but it was so damp that the old man

Mrs Remmington's shelter before being removed. Note how small it seems when compared with the grandchildren.

decided we should stay in the house. Then we got a Morrison shelter, which was an indoor one. As children we did not realize the danger we were in but our parents must have gone through hell. I remember the doodlebugs falling and then going out to collect the shrapnel.

John Radley

A Walk to School with Gas Masks

I went to Markhams Chase School soon after it opened and the war had just started. There were no buses so we walked all the way from Worthing Road but did not think anything about it but we made sure we had our gas masks. Some kids had nightmares because of the war but we were all right.

I can remember going down the Anderson shelter in our siren suits and our gas masks but it was cold. At 6 p.m. each evening we sat round the radio and listened to the news. The radio was run by an accumulator which we got charged at the shops. When we took the shelter out recently we were surprised at the thickness of the concrete.

Olive Remmington

In the Shelters

I was five when I started going to Markhams Chase School (now Janet Dukes) and when the air raid warnings went we would all line up and troop out to the shelters. We still had lessons and when we heard the all clear we returned to our classrooms. Our bungalow in Pound Lane had its roof damaged twice and other properties in the area were also damaged. They reckoned that just before the Germans crossed back across the Channel they dropped any surplus bombs in the Basildon area and I believe several people were killed in Laindon.

John Rugg

Albert Lee today.

Bombed Out

Most of the kids in Canning Town had been evacuated to different parts of the country but mum would not have it, she was determined to keep the family together. We had this place down in Basildon where we used to spend weekends and holidays. One night in London we got bombed out and I remember coming out of our air raid shelter at 4 a.m. and seeing the shattered remains of our house. The roof sagged drunkenly and all the windows were smashed. Mum, Leslie, my brother, sister Edna and our whippet dog set off with all we could salvage to our place in Basildon. On the way a fighter bomber mistook the green line bus for an army transport lorry and shot it up, damaging the roof.

We just got settled into our bungalow when our neighbours from Canning Town started to arrive. I remember their blackened faces smudged with smoke and dirt. The women had small children clinging to their legs and clutching bags and parcels. We finished up with five families living in our two-bedroomed bungalow.

Dad was conscripted into the heavy rescue and we did not see him for three weeks. The Blitz was at its height and he worked seventeen hours a day grabbing what sleep he could. When we did see him he was a changed man as he and his team were first on the scene of one of the worst incidents in the Blitz. Landsdown School was a tall building and had been hit by an aerial torpedo and had collapsed on 700 women and children while they waited to be evacuated.

One day dad was preparing to go back to London when I found a strange-looking hole about sixteen yards from the bungalow. He was in a rush and impatiently he came and looked. It was a shell hole. He cleared everybody out of the bungalow and phoned the police and I can still remember the tension as the Royal Engineer officer removed the detonator and made it safe.

Albert Lee

Extracts from Parish Magazine, 1946

Laindon War Record, Aerial Incidents 1940:

September 3rd 11 p.m. High Road and neighbouring roads 2 exploded High Explosive bombs. Gas and water mains broken. High Road blocked for several weeks and traffic diverted. In Tavistock Road 5 houses damaged. In neighbourhood 11 properties damaged.

September 5th 1 a.m. Alexandra Road, 1 unexploded high explosive bomb. 5.30 p.m. A Spitfire shot down and crashed in Markham Chase, opposite School. Pilot unhurt but machine burnt out. 9 p.m. Back of Laindon FA Post, One Unexploded high explosive bomb. 9.40 p.m. 350yds west of Fortune of War, One high explosive bomb. 9.45 p.m. Watch House Farm, One unexploded bomb.

September 8th 3.50 a.m. One unexploded bomb fell 15 Kings Road. 3.45 a.m. Two unexploded bombs Arterial Road, West of Scott's Dartboard factory. 8 a.m. Twelve incendiary bombs dropped on Jackson's Farm, Whites Bridge and Barleyland's open fields.

September 10th 3.25 a.m. One High explosive bomb Brackenmount. 4.15 am One high explosive bomb dropped on Arterial Road 400yds west of Pipps Hill. Cycle path damaged and road cracked. Gas mains broken.

September 13th Midnight 150/200 incendiary bombs, Churchill Johnson's Yard, Northumberland Avenue, Tyler's Avenue, south of Laindon, LMS

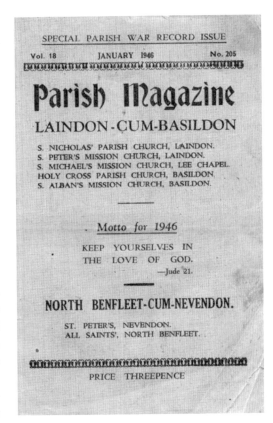

Parish Magazine, 1946.

station to Elsey Shop, Buckingham Road to St. David's Avenue.

September 15th Gladstone Road Dornier 17 plane shot down. Three enemy crew men killed. One baled out and was captured.

September 16th One unexploded high explosive bomb.

September 18th Three high explosive bombs. Wooton's Lane.

September 21st Quarter of mile from Railway Station three High Explosive bombs. 10.50pm In field west of Recreation Ground.

September 22nd One unexploded Parachute mine, Bourne Avenue behind Laindon Senior School. Elizabeth Drive/Green lane, One unexploded bomb and shrapnel.

That is just one month's extraction from the Parish Magazine.

Girl Guides looking out of Dorisdene during the Second World War.

People were Closer

During the war people were closer and there was a lot of trust. Everybody looked after everybody else and it had the effect of breaking down class barriers for the duration of the war.

Olive Remmington

The Guides could not Camp

During the war the Guides at Manor Mission were not allowed to put up tents and so mum and dad cleared all the furniture out of the large bedroom. They used the garden to have fires and cook their meals but they slept in the big bedroom.

Roy Ives

The War Agricultural Committee

I suddenly realised, when I was twelve, that there was the possibility of war. It happened while I was travelling from Laindon to Bow. Dad had just retired from the Metropolitan Police on 6 August but was recalled.

When the bombing started many weekenders came down to stay but we were evacuated to Taunton. In 1942 The War Agricultural Committee requisitioned all unused land to grow food and we were informed that our bungalow was being requisitioned for land workers. My parents had lost one house in London to bombs and had no intention of losing another to the government. So mum, my sister and I returned from Taunton. We travelled back in a very heavily laden car and were stopped at many check points especially Salisbury Plain. When we got to Laindon a young Home Guard soldier told mum that we could not go to our bungalow. My parents explained that we could not return to Taunton and had no where else to go. The Home Guard called the army, who called the police and eventually permission was given for us to stay.

Elsie Hill (*née* Neville)

Laindon Civil Defence, 1940s.

All Descended on us from London

My grandparents moved into No. 14 Brackendale Avenue just before the war. My mum and dad got married in 1942 and were going to rent a different house in the same avenue but just before they moved in a lorry load of people who had been bombed out in London, turned up on my grandparents' doorstep. Some of them were relations and the rest were friends but they had one thing in common, they had nowhere to live. My grandparents put some of them up and some moved into the house mum and dad were going to rent and the rest were put up by families all over Pitsea. Mum and dad never got the house and stayed with my grandparents.

Sandra Bonnett (*née* Keyes)

Evacuated to Buckinghamshire

I was thirteen when war broke out and was living in East Ham where I was born. The day before Chamberlain made his speech announcing that we were at war I was evacuated to Marlow in Buckinghamshire. We travelled down by train from East Ham Station. When we reached Marlow we were selected from a crowd of children and went to live in a chemist shop with a lady who had a maid and three Samoyed dogs.

The lady had a friend who owned a kennels and as I loved animals I went and helped her by walking the dogs. School was only for half a day and we shared it with the local children and I remember learning how to iron pleats.

The lady had three children who were on holiday from their private school. It was that phase in the war which was called the phoney war because nothing was happening apart from that I was homesick. After seven weeks we went home.

The people were very kind and gave us a lot of food and on my birthday they gave me my first Jeeves book. All the schools were closed and

Sandra Bonnetts' grandparents during the First World War.

then a local grammar school opened its doors to everybody but it was very haphazard and I can remember a teacher asking us what lessons we would like and I said astronomy.

The late Yvonne Smith (*née* Brasier)

Behind the Curtain

At Markham Chase School, when the air raid warning went off we would troop out in an orderly line to the shelter where we would have our lessons. If we wanted to go to the toilet we had to go behind a curtain and use a bucket.

One day a plane crashed near the school and when the all clear went the teachers let us out to have a look. I remember its tail sticking out of the ground and people coming from miles around to look at it. Surprisingly there was no

damage to the school. We did all right for food as dad grew all types of vegetables in the garden and bred rabbits, chickens and pigeons. We shared with neighbours and they with us.

Olive Remmington

Horrendous Experience

My eighteen-year-old brother joined the Navy when the war started and was in the first sea battle. He served on three ships which were attacked and sunk. His ship crept as near as it could to the Dunkirk beaches to rescue the soldiers who were struggling in the water. He said his experiences were horrendous and they changed him for life.

The late Yvonne Smith (*née* Brasier)

Bucket In The Corner

Until they got the air raid shelters in at Pitsea School we could not go and so I did not start school until I was six. The brick built shelters were dark until they put the emergency lights on. Directly the air raid warning went we were supposed to form an orderly line and file out into our own shelter but we did not, we made a dash and grabbed a seat as far away from the toilet as possible as it was just a bucket in the corner with a curtain round it.

Margaret Brown

Racing Pigeons

During the war dad bred racing pigeons for the King's Flight and was allowed special food for them. We had to keep it secret. They used pigeons to fly messages from France to England.

Olive Remmington

A German Landed

A German plane was shot down and the pilot bailed out and finished up outside the Laindon

Cinema. Everybody came out with forks, shovels, airguns or anything that was a weapon. Luckily an army car pulled up and dragged him away.

Dave Pratt

German Escaped Pilot

When a German pilot was shot down he would float down on his parachute and try to make a run for it. We had an old greyhound called Sam and kept him in a kennel, on the balcony at the back. One morning we heard him barking and somebody shouting. We thought it was a German pilot trying to creep up our back stairs but it wasn't, it was the little special constable, Mr Thompson, who had a coffee shop round the corner in Rectory Avenue. He was looking for a German pilot whose plane had been shot down and as he crept up the back stairs the dog bit him.

Margaret Browning

When the Droning Stopped

During the war I went to Canterbury Road School and when the siren went off we used to march across the playground to the shelter. When we got there the teacher used to give us a sweet. When I was eleven I went to the senior school at Catworth Street.

My sister was doing her hair with metal curlers when the air raid warning went off dad quickly ushered us all under the table. Suddenly the lights went out and somebody started to shout 'Glass! Don't move! Don't move, glass, glass!' Everybody froze not daring to move until the all clear. Then as we crawled out we found the glass. It was my sister's curlers!

I remember seeing and hearing the doodle-bugs and then, as the droning stopped, we waited with baited breath for the explosion.

Pat Radley

Prefabs

During the war they built prefabs to help with the shortage of housing and when I was seventeen we moved into one of them at the top of Kenneth Road and quite a good community built up where they all helped one another. The prefabs had a good kitchen but everything was metal and the walls were made of asbestos. They had a back boiler which heated the water, gas and electricity.

Sandra Bonnet (née Keyes)

German Prisoners Of War

There was a German prisoner of war camp up at Langdon Hills and the Germans used to help out on the farms and clear the land. Some of the local girls used to go out with them and some eventually married them. They got a lot more freedom than our lads did.

Gayle Pratt

Home Guard

When war started I wanted to join the army cadets but because I was so much bigger than everybody else, I decided that I was not going in with those little kids. I was over six feet tall and towered above them.

One day a bloke came round to Sudbury's Farm and asked 'What you doing for your country?' He told me I could join the Home Guard. He warned me that because of my age I could not use a loaded rifle and so I joined with my dad and brother. One day a warrant officer ordered us on to a lorry and took us to Harrogate firing range and ordered me to fire. I could not argue, I got two bulls-eyes out of five. When I got back to our unit and they found out, all hell let loose. What they did not realize was that I had been shooting all my life and at the age of twelve I had been knocked over by a twelve-bore shotgun.

I used to work on the farm all day and then cycle over to the post office tower at Billericay to

Left: Margaret Browning today.

Opposite: An army unit ready to go.

stand guard. We looked out for fires, planes crashing or anything like that. On Sundays we used to have mock exercises and had fire crackers on the end of our guns. We had to get from one place to another without being seen. I was only young but they had some really old people in it.

Fred Broom

Chased By Submarines

My dad was in the Merchant Navy and went to many different countries bringing back statuettes of black elephants which we had everywhere. During the war he was on the *Queen Mary* and the *Isle de France*. Most of his trips were to New York carrying troops and on more than one occasion his ship was chased by submarines but they outran them.

Dad was the ship's butcher and there was great excitement when he came home because he brought meat and sweets which were both on ration. I'll never forget a green crocheted purse with a rose pattern on it and the dolls he brought my younger sister.

Margaret Browning

She put my Sister in a Chest Of Drawers

To a five-year-old the war was quite exciting and I remember the Doodlebug that dropped over the back in Pitsea. My sister and brother had just been put to bed when we heard the moaning noise of the Doodlebug and then suddenly it stopped. There was complete silence and we held our breath as we waited for the bang. Suddenly it exploded and shook us out of bed. It fell on the little houses behind us. We were lucky it did not cause us any damage. We had quite a few Doodlebugs fall round here, one fell just over the line and all us kids trooped across to see it. It left an enormous crater. As kids one of the things we loved to do was go out and collect shrapnel.

We lived in a flat above Norton's furniture shop in the High Street but it had no shelter and so we used the one that belonged to the shop. My mum would not go down the shelter because my sister was ill but she would take me down, tuck me in and go back upstairs. It was dark and half-full of water. We had a big chest of drawers and when mum did use the shelter she would pull out one of the drawers

and put my sister in it. We also had bunk beds but you can imagine, we were surrounded by shops with nobody living in them; it was so lonely.

Dad was away in the Merchant Navy and my uncle, Robert Lyons, was in the Home Guard. There used to be an ARP post where the Pitsea clinic is now.

Margaret Browning

Dark, Dank Shelters

The war had been going for three years when I started at Pitsea School. We were regularly taken into the dark, dank air raid shelters to practise crawling out of the emergency exit on our hands and knees. I remember the wailing sirens and the relief of the all clear.

Margaret Jackson

I Took the Scholarship

During the war, my father was in the Royal Marines and my family were evacuated to Norfolk where I passed the scholarship. Two of us evacuees were offered places in Norwich Grammar School but despite everybody pleading with my mother to let me go to the school she had made up her mind to go back to Dagenham and so we returned home and I went to the South East Essex Tech.

While we were in Norfolk we were billeted with two ladies. One of them had lived in Germany and used to listen to the German radio and would rant and rave about the propaganda that was being broadcast. She offered to look after me while I was at Norwich Grammar School but mum would not hear of it.

Vic York

The Land Army

The Land Army girls moved in to clear the small plots with traction engines and chains and saws, ploughing right up to the front of empty properties, removing sheds and burning them and their contents if they fell apart and soon they created a twenty-two-acre field at the bottom of Old Hill Avenue on which they grew potatoes, peas and corn.

It became impossible to walk down to the standpipe to fetch water and so we negotiated with them so that they had half of the footpath for their tractors and we had the other half. We had to wear wellington boots which we changed at the end of the road and left under the hedge in a bag.

We helped with the harvest and gleaned the land. The prisoners of war helped the girls work on the fields and when it rained the prisoners of war would come into our house, eat their sandwiches and sing round the piano. After the war the land was not returned to the owners but was compulsorily purchased at agricultural prices.

Elsie Hill (née Neville)

Red, White And Blue Knickers

At the end of the war we children did not have a street party and were put to bed but the adults had one in the Railway Hotel, Pitsea. People were dancing and singing in the street with their red, white and blue knickers on. We crept out of bed and pressed our noses against the windows of our upstairs flat watching the grown ups go mad.

Margaret Browning

Ration Books

We lodged our ration books with Piggs of Sockets Heath because they delivered to the end of the road three days a week. On the way to school I would hang a shopping bag on a neighbour's gate with the order and money. Sometimes, at 11 a.m. we met the grocer at the end of the road. For other shopping we went to Laindon where you could buy anything from a pin to a car, there were even three cafes. I loved going into the butchers and making patterns in the sawdust on the floor.

Elsie Hall (née Neville)

The Top Shop

There was a little shop at the top of Stanley Road at the junction with Pitsea Road known as the Top Shop and it was here that my mother registered to buy wartime rationed goods.

Margaret Jackson

Nine Pence Each

During the war I used to catch rabbits with my ferrets and an ex-policeman used to buy them off me for nine pence each. He smothered them in chicken gravy and sold them as chicken meat.

Fred Broom

His Chute did not Open

One day my brother was ploughing on Sudbury's farm and because of the noise of the tractor he did not hear the siren go. Some bombs dropped in three fields right behind him. Another time we were threshing at South Green and the bloke on the stack shouted 'Get down! There's a landmine!' We looked up and there it was, coming down on its parachute. We dropped down on the stack. It blew up the house of the man that was working with me.

A bomb dropped near the Fortune of War, by the butcher's shop, I remember the massive big hole. There was one that dropped outside Toomes' office but it did not explode. Over Sudbury's Farm a German jumped out of a plane but his chute did not open and his body was like jelly.

Fred Broom

D-Day

During the war, mum my brothers and I were evacuated to Northampton but we were treated badly. We were forced to sleep on the floor and were booted out during the day. Mum could not stand it and decided she would rather go back to London and face the bombs. Two of my aunts were evacuated to Cheddington, Buckinghamshire and so mum sent us down to them while she stayed in London.

The two aunts lived in a little bungalow and worked for Coty, the perfume people. During the war the factory changed over to making shells and bullets. At weekends our friends and relations, who worked in London, came down for a night's sleep. The house used to be packed with people sleeping anywhere they could get their heads down. Not far from us was a village called Long Marston which had an aerodrome and we saw the different phases of the war through the aircraft. First there were the Wellington bombers, the Lancasters, Flying Fortresses finishing up with the Dakotas and gliders for the D-Day landings. Just before the invasion all the country lanes were taken up with army trucks and Bren gun carriers full of sleeping soldiers.

Bob Ayres

The Beginning of the End

I can remember at six years old the south side of the Arterial Road being closed and army lorries and troops with their equipment being parked along the side of the road. They were there for several weeks and it became part of life. We would go and talk to the soldiers who would give us sweets. Then one night they were gone; it was D-Day.

John Rugg

That Sally Anne Smile

It was 1946 and I breathed a sigh of relief at the thought of the war being over but I had not taken the Russians into my calculations as they tried to run us out of Berlin where I was stationed as a platoon sergeant in the Royal Norfolk Regiment.

One day we were given haversack rations for eight hours and ordered to move twenty miles outside Berlin to the edge of the Gunewald Forest where we were told to stay at all costs.

It started to rain as we arrived and started to dig in and it rained and rained. Gradually the forest turned into a sea of mud. After a day our rations ran out and we radioed for the ration lorry but were told 'Use your survival skills.' Another forty-eight hours and we were desperate as we scavenged for food, eating raw potatoes and turnips we found in a field. It still poured and I cursed when I heard on the radio that the ration lorry had tried to get through but had broken down.

We stood to on the seventh day just as dawn was breaking, pointing our rifles towards the Russian direction and trying to ignore our aching stomachs. Suddenly somebody shouted 'They're coming!' and we crouched down in silence listening to the far off sound of an engine, 'Is it a Russian tank sarg?' one of my platoon asked. I looked down at him as he crouched in the mud 'I hope not, all we've got is rifles!' 'Sarge it's over there!' 'Don't be daft, the Russians are not in that direction.' Suddenly one of our platoon shouted out 'It's the Sally Annes!' Through the rain we saw two mud-covered figures staggering in the slime leading a lorry. All the lads waved their rifles and cheered. A woman's voice cut through the forest 'Put those pop guns down and we'll get our stoves going.' We were amazed that two women had got through as the Russians raped any woman they saw. That was the best meal I've ever had and I'll never forget her smile.

I have never forgotten that meal and I have never walked past a Salvation Army box since without thinking of that time and putting something in their box.

Albert Lee

National Service: Bombing Southend Pier

When I was twenty-one I was called up for National Service. For mostly financial reasons I

A Victory party, Stacey Drive. From left to right, back row: Mrs Earl fourth from left, Phyllis Hickson, -?-, Mrs Parker, Mr Hawes, Ted Hogben, Mr Cottis, Mr Clark, Mrs Barr, Mr Cave, Mrs Cave, Mrs Doubleday, Mrs Brown, Mrs Herbert, Mrs Dean, Doreen Hawes, Margaret Lee. Second row: Valerie Album, fourth from left, Tony Fowler, Ron Herbert, seventh from left Tom Brown. Front Row: David Albury, fifth from left, Dennis Cave, eighth from left, John Cave, tenth from left, Jimmie Lee.

chose the Royal Air Force and passed the necessary exams and tests to become a flight engineer. The chance of becoming a pilot was out of the question unless I signed on for another year.

During the 1953 floods, we flew over Canvey Island and took photographs for the national papers which were printed the following day. Much to my surprise, the end of Southend Pier was used as a target for our bomb practice. Although we did not drop bombs, our navigator took photographs of the target. If it was a daylight raid we would swoop low over our bungalow with the four engines roaring.

Roy Walli

Just Finished my Apprenticeship

I got called up for my National Service directly I finished my seven-year-apprenticeship and was just starting to earn money. The National Serviceman only got eight shillings a week. I had to go down to Southend for my medical and interview with seventeen others. I was the only one that failed, because I had bad legs.

David Pratt

I Spent My Time Playing Cricket

I did my National Service in the army and was stationed at Lingfield where I played cricket most of the time. They would not even allow me to go abroad. Three times I saw my name on a list for Korea and Kenya but each time there was a big cricket match and they took me off.

Bob Ayres

RAF Padgate

In 1952 I had just finished my five years engineering apprenticeship when I received my call up papers for National Service. I went for a test in Southend. Out of thirty only two got into the RAF, the rest went into the army. On 13 October I was on my way up to RAF Padgate for my square bashing. After I finished that I was posted to Stradishall Suffolk. I finished up looking after the Wing Commander's meteor jet.

Roy Ives

Clerk In The RAF

I did my National Service in the RAF and when we arrived at Padgate for square bashing we were chased off of the lorry and our feet never touched the ground for the next six weeks. We picked up the first kit bag we saw and it took us two days to sort things out. With one or two exceptions we all pulled together. Then I was posted to Melksham. After that I was posted to Reading for my training as a clerk at Uxbridge Hospital. I was very popular because I worked in the orderly room dealing with the leave passes and railway warrants. Soon after I got demobbed I met my wife while I was on holiday in the Isle of Wight. While I was there I had a couple of letters at home recalling me. When I returned, the police came round a couple of times because I had not answered the letters. I had to go back to the forces for another two weeks.

John Snoding

Square Bashing Bridgenorth

I was called up for my national service in 1949 and joined the RAF and did my square bashing at Bridgenorth Shropshire. Those first six weeks were hard and the sergeants and corporal chased us around so our feet hardly touched the ground but they took a squad of men, some of them had two left feet, and turned them into a unit.

John Radley

Deepcut Barracks

When I did my square bashing in 1958 at the start of my National Service it was murder but I signed on for three years for the extra money. After the nightmare of trying to break the parade ground with my boots I was posted to Deepcut and trained as a driver. After my course they sent me out to Hong Kong by boat.

The cruise took us twenty-eight days and was just like a holiday camp. My cabin was a small dormitory with bunk beds. The weather was good and we spent most of the time sun-bathing but we had some Gurkhas with us who lay on their bunks being sick.

In Hong Kong our camp was next to the airport and I saw the first Comet fly in.

Roy Wallis in uniform.

John Radley square bashing in 1949.

The crowd cheered and there were loads of photographers.

All our water was piped from the mainland and in the distance you could see the Chinese peasants working in the rice fields.

The Japanese left a lot of motor equipment when they surrendered and the Army was selling it to the Chinese but we had to watch them because they would steal anything, especially sparking plugs. We used to search them as they left and would rap them over the knuckles with a pickaxe handle if they took anything.

I had a great time. The regiment had its own yacht, there were the beaches and night clubs.

Bob Garrard

John Radley's intake at Bridgenorth.

ten

Transport

Hinton's Buses

Fred Hinton and Tom Watson were pioneers of motorised buses in Laindon. They sold one of their buses to Tom Webster who operated for years in Laindon.

Ken Porter

Campbell's Buses

The buses had wooden seats, with slats. If a pregnant mother was overdue we used to say that she should have a ride on one of the buses to the Billericay Hospital. By the time she got there she would have gone into labour.

The buses were very good and stopped anywhere. You stood by the side of the road and put your arm up and they would stop. In 1944 Campbell's buses used to take us to Craylands School. We used to have Eastern National buses which went from Southend to Grays.

Margaret Browning

Station Approach

Further down, just opposite Station Approach, was Campbells Bus Co. They served the Pitsea, Vange and Basildon area for many years.

Margaret Jackson

One of Old Tom's buses, 1920s.

Coaches up Langdon Hills

Years ago all the buses were single decker because they reckoned that double-deckers could not get up Langdon Hills. Campbell's coaches mainly operated from Pitsea but here, at Laindon, we had the City Coaches and Tom Webster's buses. There were of course the steam trains.

Olive Rimmington

A Summer Ride to Southend

I remember the summer of 1957 because Laindon Link was open and my brother Barry, Martin Hale and I went out on our bikes looking for adventure .We decided to go further afield than we normally did and set off for Southend. I loved that first glimpse and smell of the sea. After a couple of hours of playing on the beach I decided I wanted to go home but the others did not so I set off on my own. I came to the incline up Laindon Link and slipped off my bike to push it. Suddenly my uncle, pulled up beside me on his Lambretta scooter and asked 'What you doing pushing it?' I was reluctant to admit to a sore bum but said I was tired .He put the bike across the back of his Lambretta while I sat on the pillion seat. As I walked through the door mum asked 'Where's your brother?' I casually replied: 'Oh I left him in Southend with Martin.' Boy when I went to bed, my backside was even sorer after 'six of the best' from dad's belt.

Brian Baylis

Buses to School

In 1947 I started to go to Mid-Essex Technical College, Chelmsford. The children who had passed the thirteen-year-old scholarships travelled there from all over the district, from Laindon, Wickford, Billericay, Pitsea and Basildon. The City Coach Co. used to run buses from Laindon Station to Billericay. The fares were a penny. We changed to the National Buses, which took us into Chelmsford. This was towards the end of the Second World War when the Doodlebugs and V2 rockets were falling out of the sky.

Roy Ives

Eastern National

When we first moved here in 1964, there was no transport. You had to go to Laindon or Pitsea for trains. Basildon Station had not been built and there were very few buses until Eastern National got their act together.

Bob Garrard

Comfort stop for Charabancs on their way to Southend during the 1950s. Note the variety of makes of coaches.

Buses to the Town Centre

In the early days we nearly always went shopping in Laindon, but for a change every so often we would go to Grays or Romford. I preferred going to Romford because we could go by train. When the shops opened in the town centre we started shopping there. We would walk to the bottom of Tyler Avenue, board the 144 service (Basildon only) or 244 service (Pitsea via Basildon) buses.

Brian Baylis

Up to London

I went up to London by train for a while with a group of friends, which proved to be really sociable. We had trouble in the seventies when we had the three-day-week and there were no trains but I got around it by driving up to Upminster and catching the tube.

Sandra Bonnett (*née* Keyes)

A Journey to the Market

During our summer holidays in the thirties we went to Wickford Market. We walked to Laindon station and took 'Old Tom's' bus to Wash Road and then walked to the White Post where we caught a City Bus to Wickford. It took

hours. In 1939 dad bought a Ford Eight and the journey was much shorter. City Buses went from London to Southend via Romford, Brentwood, Wickford and Rayleigh.

Elsie Hill (*née* Neville)

Love on the Laindon Express

Each day I travelled up to London by steam train where I worked as a secretary. The carriages used to be crammed full. That is how I met my husband during the flooding in 1953, when people from Pitsea had to get on the Laindon train. The posh passengers from Chalkwell would tie a cloth round their legs, as they imagined fleas would climb up their legs. As the uncouth youths from Laindon barged in the carriage the posh passengers would look up from their games of cards in disgust.

Olive Remmington

Railway Banks on Fire

The railway bank was always on fire near the West-Horndon-on-the-Hill signal box. Sparks and hot coal flew out from the steam trains and landed in the tall grass. The cry would go up 'Banks on fire.' We would dip a large piece of sacking in a tank of water and rush down to bash the flames out. If the fire had spread it would

Weekend traffic on its way to Southend in the late 1920s.

Bus at Basildon bus station in the town during the early 1960s.

have caught the weekenders' huts and sheds that backed on to the railway land.

One day Pete, my boy, cried out 'Mum you looked as if you were in the middle of the flames.'

Maud Sargeant

Pitsea Station

Pitsea Station was not the horrible concrete effort that there is today but a real old-fashioned station frontage, with a lovely coal fire in the booking hall and shining wooden seats where we waited for visitors from London.

Margaret Jackson

Basildon Station

When Basildon was being built there was no station in the town centre and the London, Tilbury and Southend Railway line ran trains pulled by Standard Tank 2-6-4 steam locomotives. They stopped at Laindon and Pitsea stations; passengers then had to get off and catch a bus into Basildon.

As a kid I would love to stand on the footbridge at Laindon so that when the trains roared underneath, the smoke curled up into my face and filled my lungs. It was beautiful and I still love that smell today. If ever I went missing mum and dad knew I would be in one of two

The funeral of station master Harvey, Laindon Station, believed to be the 1930s.

Cottis' bread van during the 1930s.

places, either watching the construction of Laindon Link or down at the station watching the trains.

I remember seeing a sign-post which said 'Site for Basildon Station.' It must have stood there for years before work finally started.

Brian Baylis

Other local titles published by Tempus

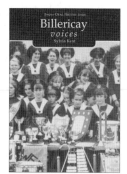

Billericay Voices
SYLVIA KENT

Billericay is much loved by its residents, and more than 80 people have contributed not only their stories, but also their photographs and other ephemera to this collection. Billericay Voices captures the essence of life in Edwardian times, through two world wars and the second half of the last century and will offer a glimpse into the lives of past inhabitants such as the famous Rosaire Circus family and evoke memories of a time that has all but vanished.

0 7524 2470 X

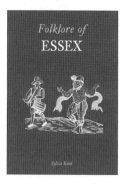

Folklore of Essex
SYLVIA KENT

Essex – the witch hunting county – is especially rich in traditions, legends, dialect and stories. It is these traditions that are gathered together in this volume and whose origins and meanings are explored to create a sense of how the customs of the past have influenced the ways of the present. Folklore of Essex will delight all those who wish to revel in the delights of times past.

0 7524 3677 5

Southend Voices
FRANCES CLAMP

This book brings together the personal memories of people who have lived and grown up in the seaside town of Southend-on-Sea during the last century. Reminiscences range from childhood games, working days and memories of the war years, to schools, churches and some of the local characters. The stories are complimented by over 120 photographs drawn from the private collections of the contributors.

07524 3215 X

Wickford Memories
JIM REEVE

Wickford has seen many changes during the last century and it is the people, whose experiences and reminiscences are recorded here, who have shaped the area into the fascinating place it is today. Illustrated with over 100 old photographs, this book brings together the personal memories of the people who have lived and worked in Wickford, vividly recalling childhood and schooldays, shops and businesses, and the war years.

0 7524 3558 2

If you are interested in purchasing other books published by Tempus, or in case you have difficulty finding any Tempus books in your local bookshop, you can also place orders directly through our website
www.tempus-publishing.com